Interactive Dictations

A Listening/Speaking/Writing Text

Judy DeFilippo
Catherine Sadow

PRO LINGUA ASSOCIATES

Pro Lingua Associates, Publishers
P.O. Box 1348
Brattleboro, Vermont 05302 USA
Office: 802 257 7779
Orders: 800 366 4775
Email: info@ProLinguaAssociates.com
WebStore www.ProLinguaAssociates.com
SAN: 216-0579

*At **Pro Lingua**
our objective is to foster an approach
to learning and teaching that we call
interplay, the **inter**action of language
learners and teachers with their materials,
with the language and culture,
and with each other in active,
creative, and productive
play.*

Copyright © 2006 by Judy DeFilippo and Catherine Sadow
For a listing of other materials under copyright, see the acknowledgements on page v.

ISBN 0-86647-197-9

Interactive Dictations was designed by Jeanne Marie Sutherland and Arthur A. Burrows. It was set in Palatino, the most widely used, and pirated, face of the twentieth century, which was designed by Hermann Zapf in 1948 in Frankfurt. Although modern, it is based on Renaissance designs typical of the Palatinate area in Germany. The illustrated proverb on page 158 is © 2002 by Patrick R. Moran from *Lexicarry.* The clipart illustrating the book is from The Big Box of Art, Copyright © 2001 Hemera Technologies Inc., and Art Explosion 750,000 Images, Copyright © 1995-2000 Nova Development Corporation. The book was printed and bound by Sheridan Books in Chelsea, Michigan.

Printed in the United States of America
First printing 2006. 1000 copies in print.

Contents

Contents ❀

❀ *Acknowledgements* ❀

The authors based many of their activities on concepts introduced by P. Davis and M. Rinvolucri, who co-authored ***Dictation, New Methods, New Possibilities,*** Cambridge University Press, 1988.

The authors are grateful to the authors, publishers, and others who have given permission to reprint copyrighted materials:

> **The Academy of Achievement:** Amy Tan interview
>   http//www.achievement.org
> **Cartoon Stock:** *Chocoholics*
> **The Hingham Journal:** *The Noblest of Professions* by Cathy Conley
> **The Boston Globe:** *Eat that Insect?* by Jessica Kowal
> **The New York Times**: *How Honest Are You?* by N. Onishi
> **The Chicago Tribune:** *Dear Amy* by A. Dickinson
> Anonymous Internet Sources
>   *Privacy*
>   *Dear Mom and Dad*
>   *Made ... Where?*

The authors wish to thank the following teachers who field-tested the text and gave valuable feedback:

> **Daniel Doherty,** Immigrant Learning Center, Malden, MA
> **Shirley Taylor,** SCALE, Somerville, MA
> **Laura Brooks,** SCALE, Somerville, MA
> **Liz Nicholson,** Showa Boston Institute
> **Debby Fitzpatrick,** Showa Boston Institute
> **Katharine Doubtit,** Showa Boston Institute

For our grandchildren

Courtney
Connor
Eli
Zachary

Introduction

Interactive Dictations is a low intermediate to intermediate level text that is intended to improve the listening, speaking, and writing skills of ESL students. Reading skills are also reinforced, along with attention to vocabulary and grammar. This text provides a wide variety of dictations that include provocative news items, problems to solve, and decisions to make. Each dictation naturally leads to a discussion activity that can take twenty to thirty minutes.

Teachers can pick and choose which dictations meet the needs, interests, and levels of their particular students. Dictations are classified by topic, but one topic is not necessarily easier or harder than another. Topics can be used to supplement a theme or grammar point of an existing text. There are seven topic areas.

Within topics, the units are designed to stand alone — each unit contains one dictation activity, a follow-up discussion, and a writing activity. Pair or small group work is encouraged in both the dictation and discussion sections. This text includes several cooperative learning and role-play activities.

Some units are short. Teachers can use these as fill-ins for a 15 to 30 minute lesson. Longer units will take 30 to 60 minutes.

The full dictations are available in the second part of the book. A CD with the full dictations is also available.

❀ Different Types of Dictation ❀

Dictation has been presented in many forms through the years in reading, listening, grammar, and writing classes. It is also used as an assessment procedure. This text, however, does not deal with scoring or analyzing student work. The dictations are meant to be a challenging springboard to discussion and writing by which the students are encouraged to use the language they have just encountered in the dictation.

This text includes five forms of dictation: partial, pair, dictogloss, prediction, and note taking. While all units include pair and group work in the discussion segments, several units will include more extensive cooperative and role-play types of activities. See the unit on proverbs as an example.

Partial (sometimes known as *cloze*)

Most of the dictations in this text are partial dictations where words, phrases, or chunks of language have been deleted, and students are required to listen and write down the missing words. All the dictations should be discussed upon completion. Pair work is encouraged.

Pair (sometimes known as mutual)

This dictation requires students to work in pairs to combine two-part texts into one continuous piece. One student has a copy of dictation "Student A," and the other has dictation "Student B." Each student has half of the text. They should not look at each other's sheets. Student A dictates and Student B writes, then B dictates and A writes, and so on until the story is complete.

Dictogloss

In this kind of dictation, the focus is on getting the gist or main idea of a sentence or short paragraph.

There are many variations of the dictogloss technique. In the directions for the sentence level dictogloss, students are told that they will hear a sentence only once, after which they are to jot down the words they can recall and try to reconstruct the sentence in writing as accurately as they can. The first time this is done, the teacher will probably have to allow the students a second reading until they discover that they need to pay attention the first time around. As the students work at rebuilding the sentence, they can work in pairs and then fours.

Also included are very short paragraphs to be dictated. In this kind of dictation, the students should focus more on the meaning of the paragraph than on the individual sentences; they are not expected to get everything word for word. The teacher may read the paragraph once at normal speed while the students just listen; then the teacher can read it again with longer pauses between sentences if necessary. The students write only one sentence which expresses the main idea of the entire paragraph.

Prediction

Prediction lessons come in two parts. The first part focuses more on reading skills and grammar. The students are required to work in pairs, reading the passage and predicting (or guessing) what should be in each blank space. Any logical or grammatically correct word or phrase can be accepted. Part Two requires the students to listen to the same passage and see if their guesses were correct, or similar.

Note Taking

Note taking activities require students to write down information they think is important for the discussion that follows. This may only amount to a few words; however, when students work in pairs after the listening section is over, they should compare their notes to a partner's to be sure they caught the pertinent information. When this is accomplished, they are able to discuss the issues that follow.

❀ Tips for Teachers ❀

1. When reading the full dictations, try to speak naturally, at normal speed, keeping the features of the spoken language. If you are reading the full text at normal speed and you know the exercise will be fairly easy for your students, give the word, phrase, or chunk of language only once. Try to start with a pace that is comfortable for your students, and then make them work a bit at understanding. If you think the text will be difficult for your students, repeat two, possibly three times. When field testing our material, several teachers said that they thought the material looked quite difficult for their students, but they were surprised how well their students did. It's up to you to decide what works best. If you have to repeat more than three times, the text is too difficult for your students.

2. The students may want to check the spelling of a word or words as you are giving the dictation. It's best to tell them to wait until the end of the activity.

3. For numbers, have the students write numerals, rather than the word (15, instead of fifteen), except for single-digit numbers (1-9). They should also use dollar ($) and percentage (%) symbols rather than writing out the words.

4. One key to making the dictation a positive experience is to have students correct their own work. When the dictation is completed, the students check with each other in pairs on what they've heard, while you walk around helping and clarifying. This, in itself, allows for a great deal of discussion. After they have self-corrected, they can turn to the full dictation texts for confirmation. You can then go over the dictation with the class and discuss whatever vocabulary or concepts they don't understand.

5. Rather than read the full dictations from the appendix, you may find it helpful to copy the page you're dictating and fill in the blanks yourself ahead of time. This is helpful when giving feedback. It's easier when you're working from the same page as your students. Here is an example from "Proverbs:"

    1. There's no *place like home.*

    2. Don't *count your chickens* before they are hatched.

6. There was no one pattern that was followed when choosing words or phrases to be deleted. Sometimes the deletions focus on idioms, sometimes on numbers, sometimes grammar, sometimes vocabulary.

7. *Interactive Dictations* also works well for substitute teachers, since a minimum amount of preparation is needed.

8. You and your students can also create dictations from local newspapers, the Internet, or any other source. This way you can choose a timely topic and easily adapt it to the level of your students.

9. With higher level students, you may want to ask a student to give a full dictation. The reader may prepare for this by listening to the CD.

10. Discussions. The discussions can be by pairs, small groups, or the entire class.

11. Cooperative activities have been included in four of the units. These are extensions of pair and group work and they are one of the best ways to have everyone in the class very involved.

Day 1. There are four groups, A,B,C, and D. On Day 1, everyone in each group is responsible for researching part of the material assigned to that group.

Day 2. All groups reassemble, and the group members go over all the information they have gathered, being sure that each member is fully familiar with all the material.

Day 2 or 3. New groups are formed. Each group includes one person from each of the original groups. In other words, each new group will consist of one A, one B, one C, and one D. The Group A person is responsible for sharing all of the Group A material. By the end of this activity every member of the class should have the complete information. This can be a lengthy activity, but it is very valuable, especially for shyer students.

❀ Using the CD ❀

Although it is not necessary to have and use the accompanying CD, many teachers find that having the CD provides greater flexibility in using the material. It can be used in several ways:

1. Play the track once through without stopping **before** reading the dictation to the students. This will introduce the topic and give the students a head start toward comprehending the dictation when it is read to them.

2. To give the students a chance to hear a different voice, have the students take the dictation from the CD. Although more challenging, this can help the students prepare for standardized listening tests. You can use the pause button; that will allow the students time to fill in the blanks.

3. Play the CD **after** the students have taken the dictation and checked their answers. This can help the students improve and become more confident in listening comprehension.

On the CD, each dictation text is on a separate track. The CD track numbers are given in the table of contents of this book (iii-iv), and also next to the titles of the gapped texts (1-130) and the titles of full dictations texts (131-166).

❀ Using a Listening Laboratory ❀

Almost any dictation that is done in class can also be done in the language lab. However, there are some additional things that can be done in the lab that cannot be done in the classroom.

1. Read a short partial dictation in the lab. Then have the students tape what they have written. You can collect both, and then on the student tape give some feedback on their pronunciation.

2. The students create their own partial dictation and make four or five copies of it. They record it carefully and leave the results at their stations. They then move from station to station doing four or five of each other's dictations. The students' dictations can follow a general theme – food, for example – or a specific form – a joke or poem.

3. Dictate a chunk of language. The students listen and record it. Add another chunk. The students record again. At the end of the short, fairly simple dictation, the students transcribe it. Collect their transcriptions and make appropriate comments and corrections.

4. Dictate a problem. An example might be a "Dear Abby" that you have turned into a dictation. After each student has done the dictation, they record the solution to the problem. You should listen and respond to the solution, or the students can move from station to station listening to their fellow students and making comments of agreement or disagreement. By preparing short, easy-to-understand dictations first, you can also use this technique to introduce current political or social topics that you think will be of particular interest to your students.

❀ About the Full Dictation Texts ❀

The complete texts of the dictations begin on page 131. You can read these full texts to give the dictations, have a student read them, or use the CD.

Interactive Dictations

Made. . . Where?

full text on page 132 (cd track 1)

Introduction ❀

Can you guess what percent of Americans own foreign cars? Can you guess which foreign car company sells the most cars in the U.S.? Do you know why some Americans refuse to buy a foreign car?

Vocabulary ❀

1. **perking** - (short for percolating) - passing a liquid through a filter
2. **discouraging** - leading to a loss of hope or confidence
3. **fruitless** - useless; without benefit
4. **sandals** - simple footwear, usually with straps instead of a top with laces
5. **pour** - to let flow
6. **wonder** - to have an interest in knowing

Pair dictation ❈

In this dictation work in pairs and dictate to each other. Student A (page 2) has half of the paragraph and reads their lines to Student B, who has the other half (A dictates and B writes). Then Student B (page 3) dictates and A writes until the paragraph is complete. When you are finished, check your paragraph with your partner.

❈ Student A ❈

Bill Smith started _____ _____ _____. He set his alarm clock (_____ ___ _____)

for six o'clock a.m. While his coffeepot (_____ ___ _____) was perking, he shaved with his

_____ _____ (_____ ___ _____ _____). He put on a dress shirt (_____

___ _____ _____), designer jeans (_____ ___ _____), _____ _____

_____ (made in Korea).

After he cooked _____ _____ ___ ____ _____ _____ _____

(made in India), he sat down with his calculator (_____ ___ _____) to see how much ___

_____ _____ _____.

After he set his watch (made in Taiwan) ___ _____ _____ (made in India), ___ _____ ____

_____ _____ (made in Germany) and _____ _____ _____ for a good-paying

American job. ___ _____ _____ ___ _____ _____ discouraging and fruitless day, Bill

_____ ___ _____ for a while. He put on his sandals (_____ ___ _____),

poured himself a _____ ___ _____ (made in France), and _____ ___ _____ ____

(_____ ___ _____), and then wondered why ___ _____ _____ ____

_____-_____ _____ in America!

Pair dictation ❋

In this dictation work in pairs and dictate to each other. Student A (page 2) has half of the paragraph and reads their lines to Student B, who has the other half (A dictates and B writes). Then Student B (page 3) dictates and A writes until the paragraph is complete. When you are finished, check your paragraph with your partner.

❋ Student B ❋

_____ _____ _____ the day early. ____ _____ _____ _____ _____

(made in Japan) _____ ____ ___ _____ ___ ___ . _____ _____ _____

(made in China) _____ _____ ____ _____ _____ _____ electric razor (made in

Hong Kong). ____ _____ ___ _____ _____ _____ (made in Sri Lanka) _____

_____ (made in Singapore), and tennis shoes (_____ ___ _____).

_____ ___ _____ his breakfast in his new elecric fryer (_____ ___ _____),

___ _____ _____ _____ _____ _____ (made in Mexico) ___ _____ _____

_____ he could spend today.

_____ ___ _____ _____ _____ (_____ ___ _____) to the radio (_____

___ _____), he got in his car (_____ ___ _____) _____ continued his search _____

____ _____ - _____ _____ _____ . At the end of yet another _____

_____ _____ _____ _____, _____ decided to relax _____ ___ _____. ___

_____ ___ _____ _____ (made in Brazil), _____ _____ ____ glass of

wine (_____ ___ _____), _____ turned on the TV (made in Indonesia), _____ _____

___ _____ _____ he couldn't find a good-paying job ____ _____!

Discussion ❈ *Discuss these questions with a partner. Share your ideas with the class.*

1. From the dictation you can see that the U.S. imports products from all over the world. How does this affect the job market in the U.S? Why are some products produced in other countries when it is possible to make them in the U.S? Do you know what the minimum wage is in the U.S?

2. What countries export these products? If you aren't sure, guess! You can name more than one country.

coffee _____   tea _____   shoes _____   oil _____

airplanes _____   cars _____   potatoes _____   beer _____

beef _____   rice _____   diamonds _____   wine _____

clothes _____   oranges _____   bananas _____   gold _____

Idioms and Expressions ❈ *Talk about the meanings of these expressions.*

She has a lot of get up and go.

Clothes make the man.

He always has a beef about something.

If the shoe fits, wear it.

He went bananas when he heard the news that she is now the top banana in the company.

She has a heart of gold, and she's worth her weight in gold.

The students burned the midnight oil before the exam.

The topic of the death penalty is a hot potato for politicians.

Writing ❈ *Tourism is a major industry in many countries, especially those with tropical climates. Talk, then write about a place in the world you would like to visit and explain why. Here are some possibilities:*

Hawaii, London, Paris, Tokyo, Bali, Fiji Islands,
Rome, Puerto Rico, Montreal, Istanbul, Beijing,
Taipei, Cairo, Mexico, Rio de Janeiro.

Taxes and Take-Home Pay

full text on page 133 (cd track 2)

Introduction ❋

The United States imposes different kinds of taxes on its citizens: income taxes, sales taxes, social security taxes, property taxes, cigarette taxes, and many more. What kinds of taxes do you pay? Talk about it with the class.

Vocabulary ❋

1. **federal income tax** - a percentage of your salary that you pay to the U.S. government
2. **state income tax** - a percentage of your salary that you pay to the state government
3. **social security (FICA) tax** - a percentage of your salary that goes to older and non-working people
4. **pension** - payments by a business or government to retired people
5. **benefits** - positive job extras (medical insurance, pension fund, etc.)

Dictation ❋

Listen and fill in the blanks. Then decide if the statement about taxes is true or false. Correct and discuss the dictation with a partner. Guess if you don't know! Many Americans don't know!

___ 1. An average American working couple pays _____% of their _____ _____ in

taxes every year.

___ 2. If you make _____ _____ _____ a year, you do not have to pay taxes.

___ 3. The United States is the country with _____ _____ _____.

___ 4. _____ _____ _____ can affect the amount of tax you pay.

___ 5. Married and middle-aged people pay more in income tax than the _____ _____

_____.

___ 6. People with a salary between _____ and _____ pay more to

the government than people who make more than $50,000.

___ 7. People who make the same income pay _____ _____ _____ of income tax.

Discussion ❋ *Read the information and discuss the questions below with a partner.*

Here is the pay stub for Nina Goodman, who works at the Acme Company. She gets paid every two weeks. Her take-home pay for that time period is $713.91.

Regular salary:	$1295.16
Pension	103.61
Medical Insurance	102.89
Income Tax	229.24
Social Security Tax	91.21
State Income Tax	54.30
Take-home pay (net)	$713.91

1. How many different taxes does she pay?
2. What is her yearly salary?
3. Why is it important to have medical insurance?
4. What other benefit is important to employees?
5. What does "net" mean?
6. Is life insurance taken out of her salary?
7. Social security is a federal retirement fund. When will she get this money back?

Writing ❋ *Find out what a graduated tax means and how it is different from a flat-rate tax. Write a paragraph about this.*

Do You Want to Be a Nurse?

full text on page 134 (cd track 3)

Introduction ❋

Children often want to be firefighters, pilots, or actors when they grow up. As they grow older they choose professions that are less dangerous and more realistic. What did you want to be when you were a child? Here is some advice for a woman who is thinking of becoming a nurse. Listen to the advantages and disadvantages of the nursing profession.

Vocabulary ❋

1. **impact** - effect or influence
2. **24/7** - all day and night, all week (pronounced twenty-four seven)
3. **commitment** - a promise to do something or behave in a particular way
4. **mandatory** - required
5. **overtime** - time that is spent working in a job in addition to the normal working hours
6. **shift** - time of work, for example: 9-5 or 12-8
7. **bodily fluids** - body liquids like blood and saliva
8. **unreasonable** - wrong, unfair
9. **rehabilitation** - helping someone to live a healthy, active life after a sickness or injury
10. **on the plus side** - as an advantage, an asset
11. **stuck** - unable to move forward
12. **options** - things that you can choose to do in a particular situation
13. **pediatrics** - medical care for children

Prediction Dictation ❋

In this dictation you are not going to listen first. Work with a partner and fill in each blank with a word you think is correct. When you are finished, you will listen and do the dictation on the next page. Then compare your responses.

Nurse: I think it's great that you _____ considering nursing as a career, but I would look _____ closely at the impact it can have on your personal _____. I don't _____ to be negative, _____ a lot of people look at _____ as a well-paying _____ without finding out what the job really ____. Nursing is a 24/7 commitment. We are expected to _____ weekends and _____, and there is a mandatory overtime in some facilities. This means if _____ second shift calls in sick, _____have to stay to cover the floor. You may _____ always get the vacation you request. You _____ two children; are you prepared ____ _____ Christmas and _____? You will be expected ____. _____ been a nurse for 25 _____ , and I couldn't see myself doing _____ _____ . However, nursing is not for _____. You _____ ____ deal with very ill people, bodily fluids, unreasonable families _____ doctors, and it can be very stressful at times. However, on the plus side, you do _____ a difference in people's lives, and it's _____to see them get well. Also it's possible to _____ the area of your work. You _____do home care, intensive care, rehabilitation, pediatrics, maternity, or – that is the great thing _____ nursing – you aren't stuck doing the same _____. There are always other options.

Listening Dictation ❋

Listen and fill in the blanks with the word you hear. Then with a partner, compare your prediction to the listening.

Nurse: I think it's great that you _____ considering nursing as a career, but I would look _____ closely at the impact it can have on your personal _____. I don't _____ to be negative, _____ a lot of people look at _____ as a well-paying _____ without finding out what the job really ____. Nursing is a 24/7 commitment. We are expected to _____ weekends and _____, and there is a mandatory overtime in some facilities. This means if _____ second shift calls in sick, _____have to stay to cover the floor. You may _____ always get the vacation you request. You _____ two children; are you prepared ____ _____ Christmas and _____? You will be expected ____. _____ been a nurse for 25 _____, and I couldn't see myself doing _____ _____. However, nursing is not for _____. You _____ ____ deal with very ill people, bodily fluids, unreasonable families _____ doctors, and it can be very stressful at times. However, on the plus side, you do _____ a difference in people's lives, and it's _____to see them get well. Also it's possible to _____ the area of your work. You _____do home care, intensive care, rehabilitation, pediatrics, maternity or – that is the great thing _____ nursing – you aren't stuck doing the same _____. There are always other options.

Discussion ❋ *Discuss these questions with a partner. Share your ideas with the class.*

1. What does the writer say are the advantages and disadvantages of being a nurse? Can you think of any others that are not mentioned?
2. In recent years more and more nurses are men. Can you think of any reasons for this?
3. Are you suited to nursing? Would you be a good nurse? Why?
4. The writer mentions pediatrics. Pediatrics is the medical specialty dealing with children, and the doctor is called a pediatrician. Here are five other specialties. Find out what they mean and then add three of your own to share with the class.

Specialty	Doctor	What is it?
1. obstetrics	obstetrician	
2. surgery	surgeon	
3. dermatology	dermatologist	
4. cardiology	cardiologist	
5. orthopedics	orthopedist	
6.		
7.		
8.		

Cooperative Learning ✾

Work in 3 or 4 groups with 3, 4, or 5 students in a group. Each person in the group finds out what one or several of these people do and then reports back to their group. This can be done as homework or classwork. Each person in the group must be prepared to learn and tell all the information. Then all groups share what they have learned in newly reconfigured groups.

Group 1
- Receptionist
- Umpire
- Accountant
- Dramatist
- Bus boy
- Crane operator

Group 3
- Plumber
- Head of State
- Mason
- Architect
- Antiques dealer
- Orthodontist

Group 2
- Cab driver
- Computer analyst
- Sous chef
- Social worker
- Consul
- Linguist

Group 4
- Butcher
- Headmistress
- Massage therapist
- Probation officer
- Exterminator
- Maitre d'

Writing ❋ *Write about the advantages and disadvantages of a job you have now, or a job you've had in the past, or a job you'd like to have.*

Buying a Used Car
full text on page 135 (cd track 4)

Introduction ❀

Most people who buy a car, new or used, do not pay cash. They go to a bank and take out a car loan. Who you are, your job history, and credit record are all important. Here are three permanent residents who want to buy a used car. After you have the necessary information about these people, decide if they can afford to buy one.

Vocabulary ❀

1. **utility** - any basic service such as electricity, gas, running water
2. **down payment** - a partial payment at the time of buying something
3. **credit record** - a history of how you spend your money and pay your bills
4. **loan** - money that you borrow at a rate of interest
5. **interest rate** - a percentage paid on an amount of money
6. **take-home pay** - the money you take home after taxes and other deductions
7. **car insurance** - an agreement with a company in which the company will pay for a loss or accident
8. **scholarship** - a loan or a grant that pays for study

Note Taking ❀

Listen and write the information about each person. Then work with a partner, check your notes with each other, and decide who can afford to buy a car.

Paulina, from Brazil, age 27

How long in U.S.? _____	Price of used car	_____	
How long-driving? _____	20% down payment	_____	
Present salary _____	% of interest	_____	
Take-home pay _____	Credit record?	_____	
Monthly expenses _____	Monthly payment	_____ (3 years)	
	Car insurance/month	_____	

Sammy, from Lebanon, age 22

How long in U.S.? _____	Price of used car	_____	
How long driving? _____	20% down payment	_____	
Present salary _____	% of interest	_____	
Take-home pay _____	Credit record?	_____	
Monthly expenses _____	Monthly payment	_____ (5 years)	
	Car insurance/month	_____	

Ashvin, from India, age 19

How long in U.S.? _____   Price of used car   _____

How long driving?_____   20% down payment   _____

Part-time salary   _____   % of interest   _____

Co-signer of loan   _____   Credit record   _____

Monthly expenses _____   Monthly payment   _____

                                            Car insurance/month _____

Discussion ❀ *Discuss these situations with a partner and decide what to do. Share your ideas with the class.*

1. Karl is looking at two used cars that he can afford. Which one should he buy? Why?

Chevy Cavalier (3 years old)	Toyota Corolla (2 years old)
Price: $9000	Price: $9500
Mileage: 25,000	Mileage: 30,000
One-year warranty	One-year warranty

2. Rita, mother of three, can afford a new van. Which one should she buy? Why?

Honda Odyssey	Ford Freestar
Price: $25,000	Price: $21,000
Miles per gallon: 35	Miles per gallon: 20
Safety record: Excellent	Safety record: Good

Discussion ❋ *Discuss these questions with a partner. Then share your ideas with the class. Your teacher will give you the answers.*

1. Guess the names of the top five car companies, domestic and foreign, that Americans prefer.

   _____   _____   _____   _____   _____

2. Of the top five, which do you think would be the top three in sales and in quality?

   _____   _____   _____

3. Guess the car and model that has been the best seller in the U.S. for several years.

   _____

4. What car features are important when you buy a car, new or used?
   miles per gallon   automatic/standard shift   color
   style   speed   air conditioning   comfort

5. Last year, the price of a Toyota Camry and a Honda Accord was approximately the same. If you shop around from dealer to dealer, you can often save $1000 or more.

6. How do people usually buy a car – from a dealer, from classified ads, or from friends? Explain.

7. Look at the used car ads in the automotive section of your local newspaper. Decide on a car that you might like to buy. Bring the ad to class and discuss it with a partner. Decide what questions you would ask the seller.

Writing ❋ *Write a paragraph about your "dream" car, truck, or motorcycle.*

Privacy
full text on page 136 (cd track 5)

Introduction ❋

Frank's son, age 10, received a pre-approved credit card in the mail. Frank, very surprised, traced this offer back to a national athletic organization that was in charge of a swimming program that his son was in. Frank was angry that this organization would sell the names and addresses of these young people, and he took his son out of the program. This is only one of the ways we lose our right to privacy.

Vocabulary ❋

1. **privacy** - a condition of being able to keep your own affairs secret
2. **pre-approved** - already okayed
3. **trace** - to find the origins of something in a place, time, or action
4. **multi-** - many
5. **How come?** - Why?
6. **blood pressure** - the force with which blood travels through your body
7. **cholesterol** - a chemical substance found in fat, blood, and other cells in your body which scientists think may cause heart disease
8. **soybean** - the bean of an Asian plant from which oil and food containing a lot of protein is produced
9. **local** - connected with a particular place or area, especially the place you live in
10. **over the limit** - too much
11. **based on** - a point from which to develop an idea or plan
12. **@#$@&?#** - a substitute for bad, abusive language
13. **I give up** - "You win; I won't argue anymore."
14. **By the way** - incidentally (used to introduce a new subject)
15. **diabetic** - a person who has diabetes, a disease in which there is too much sugar in the blood

Dictation ✽

Fill in the blank space with the word you hear. With a partner, correct and discuss the dialogue. Was this dialogue funny?

Operator: Thank you for calling Pizza Castle. May I _____ _____ _____?

Customer: Hello, can I order...........

Operator: Can I have your multi-purpose _____ _____ first, sir?

Customer: It's eh .... hold on .... 3122058889-31-_____.

Operator: Okay ... _____ Mr. Saxe and _____ _____from 26 Rose

                    Lane. Your home number is 627-734-_____. Your office is 627-373-5716 and

                    your mobile is 627-266-_____. Would you like to have this delivery made to 26

                    Rose Lane?

Customer: Yes. How did you get all my phone numbers?

Operator: We are connected ____ _____ _____, sir.

Customer: May I order your _____ _____?

Operator: That's _____ ____ _____ _____, sir.

Customer: How come?

Operator: _____ ____ your medical records, you have _____ blood pressure

                    and even _____ cholesterol level, sir.

Customer: What do you recommend then?

Operator: Try our low-fat soybean yogurt pizza. _____ _____ ____.

Customer: How do you _____ _____ _____?

Operator: You _____ a book titled "Popular Soybean Yogurt Dishes" from your

                    local library last week, sir.

Customer: Okay, I _____ ____. Give me three family-sized ones, then. How much will that

                    cost?

Operator: That should be enough for _____ _____ ____ _____ , sir. The total is

                    _____.

Customer: _____ ____ _____ by credit card?

Operator: _____ _____ _____ you have to pay us cash, sir. Your credit card is over

                    the limit and you've owed your bank _____ since October.

Customer: I guess I'll have to run to the neighborhood ATM and _____ _____

before your guy arrives.

Operator: You can't do that, sir. Based on the records, _____ _____ your

daily limit on machine withdrawal today.

Customer: _____ _____. Just send the pizzas. I'll have the cash ready. _____ _____

is it going to take?

Operator: _____ ___ _____, sir, but if you can't wait, you can always come

and collect it on your motorcycle.

Customer: Wha.............!

Operator: _____ ____ the details in the system, you own a Harley, registration

number E1123.

Customer: @# %$@&#

Operator: Better watch your language, sir. Remember that on _____ ____ you were accused

of using abusive language to an officer.

Customer: (Speechless)

Operator: Is there _____ _____?

Customer: Nothing. ____ _____ _____, aren't you going to give me three bottles of Pepsi?

Operator: We normally would, sir, but based on your records, you're also _____.

Discussion ❊

1. After you've corrected and discussed this dictation, read it aloud, with your partner taking one part and you taking the other part.
2. How much information do you think can be found out about you? Does this bother you?
3. What has made this possible? Is there anything we can do about it?

Writing ❊

 Write a paragraph about the man in this dialogue. Describe everything you know about him. Mr. Saxe, who lives at.........................

Pocket Translators

full text on page 138 (cd track 6)

Introduction ❖

Many ESL teachers worry about students using pocket translators too often in ESL classrooms. One teacher asked her colleagues on an ESL chat line to give their opinions about the advantages and disadvantages of allowing students to use them in class. She received many answers. Most of the teachers agreed that students use them too often. But do students agree?

Vocabulary ❖

1. **pocket translators** - small computer bilingual dictionaries
2. **chat line** - an internet site where people with similar interests share opinions
3. **colleagues** - people who work together or people who work in the same field
4. **a last resort** - the last thing you should do
5. **stumbling block** - something that makes it difficult for you to reach a goal
6. **to move on** - to go on to the next thing

Dictogloss ❖

Listen to a complete sentence only once and write down the words you can remember. With a partner try to reconstruct the sentence in writing as accurately as possible.Then decide whether or not you agree or disagree with each sentence. (A-agree, D-Disagree)

_____1.

_____2.

_____3.

_____4.

_____5.

Discussion ❖ *Discuss these questions with a partner.*

Here is one teacher's answer from the ESL chat line, "In an ESL class, pocket translators are the last resort. If you can't guess the word, can't understand the teacher's explanation, can't understand the definition in your dictionary, can't get any help from your classmates, then maybe it's time to use it. But translating all the time isn't good language practice."

1. Do you agree with the point of view?
2. Does your teacher let you use one in class?
3. Teachers say that you should use one in your math class or your history class. What is the difference?
4. Poll your classmates to see how many of them frequently use a pocket translator in class and why. What are the most common reasons for using them?

Writing ❖

Students should not use a pocket translator (or a bilingual dictionary) in class. Do you agree or disagree?

The Noblest of Professions

full text on page 138 (cd track 7)

Introduction ❖

Every September teachers return to their classooms ready to welcome a new group of students for the coming year. And every June they send their beloved students on to their next adventure. For a six-year-old, it means going into second grade. For a high school senior, it may mean college or a full-time job. And for college graduates who have majored in education, it means the beginning of the noblest of professions. Teaching!

Vocabulary ❖

1. **guide** - leader
2. **counselor** - advisor
3. **measure** - to find the size, weight, speed, etc.
4. **cheerleader** - a person who leads a crowd in support of a team
5. **self-esteem** - liking oneself, a sense of self-worth
6. **optometrist** - an eye doctor who examines eyes and writes prescriptions for glasses
7. **comedian** - a person who entertains others by using humor
8. **psychiatrist** - a medical doctor who works with people who are having mental problems

Dictation ❖

Here's what one writer has to say about teachers. Write the word or words you hear in the blank spaces. Discuss with a partner. Which ones do you like?

1. A teacher is a guide in the _____ ____ _____.

2. A teacher is a _____. The product is _____.

3. A teacher is a _____, a _____, a healer of broken hearts.

4. A teacher is ____ _____ _____ than what a test can measure.

5. A teacher is a coach, a cheerleader, _____ ____ _____.

6. A teacher is a psychiatrist fostering _____-_____ and an optometrist

   helping students _____ _____.

7. A teacher is an _____, a _____, and a storyteller.

8. A teacher is an X-ray technician _____ _____, a publisher at the copy

   machine, a partner _____ _____ in the adventure of education.

Discussion ❖

Discuss the following items with a partner. Then share your ideas with the class.

1. What are some qualities of a good _____?
   a. teacher   b. student   c. accountant   d. parent

2. Rank these jobs according to how well-paid you think they are in the United States.

   Which jobs do not require a university degree?

   ___ airline pilot   ___ registered nurse   ___ electrician

   ___ mail carrier   ___ surgeon   ___ electrical engineer

   ___ criminal lawyer   ___ psychologist   ___ plumber

3. How happy are people with their jobs? Here are some comments that people make about their jobs. Which ones do you agree with and why?

   "I like working on a team."   "I like working alone."

   "I like to travel a lot."   "I'd go crazy sitting behind a desk all day."

   "I'm my own boss."   "There are lots of opportunities for advancement."

   "I get a good feeling of   "The hours are flexible."
   accomplishment."

4. Here are the top ten most dangerous jobs in the U.S. Can you guess which are the top five?

   timber cutters   laborers   construction laborers

   truck drivers   carpenters   farm occupations

   groundskeepers   airplane pilots   sales occupations

   police and detectives

Writing ❖

What are some qualities of a good teacher? Before you write your paragraph, read the following items and if you agree, include some or all of them in your composition. Explain why you chose the items.

A good teacher

- explains clearly
- knows the subject very well
- is strict
- cares about the students
- knows the answers to all of the students' questions
- prepares you for state tests
- is friendly, patient, and kind
- makes students figure out problems for themselves

Opportunity Knocks

full text on page 139 (cd track 8)

Introduction ❖

A newly arrived immigrant had an opportunity, took it, and was successful.

Vocabulary ❖

1. **traumatized** - not able to do things normally because of a very bad experience
2. **mentor** - an experienced person who advises, encourages, and helps a less
    experienced person
3. **to turn down** - to refuse
4. **kidnapped** - taken against your will
5. **scholarship** -   money given for education either for excellence or need

Prediction Dictation ❖

In this activity you are not going to listen first. Work with a partner and fill in each blank with a word you think is correct. When you are finished, you will listen and do the dictation on the next page. Then compare your responses.

Most _____ schools will not accept young people who are _____ 17, have a history of school troubles, speak little _____ , or otherwise seem unlikely to be able ____ _____ the final exams and graduate in a reasonable amount of _____. ____ New York, a night _____day school _____ created for these students.

Four_____ ago, just before his sixteenth _____, Jean-Luc Gerard landed at Kennedy _____with $20.00 in his _____, alone, speaking no _____, and traumatized by the deaths of his uncle and brother in a West African civil war. _____ mother _____kidnapped, and he _____ saw her again.

Four _____ later Mr. Gerard _____ graduated from this high school with a full _____ to Dartmouth College. He had been a night student while _____ full-time during the _____. The teachers helped _____ with tutoring. They _____ him English. They _____ him with immigration and gave him a mentor. The mentor even gave him a party when he was _____ to college.

More than half the students at the _____are recent _____ like Mr. Gerard. Most come to school during the day for intensive _____ classes after they have been turned down by other high schools because of their age. No one at the school has much _____. Many students at the school hold some kind of _____ to support _____, their children, and sometimes other family _____.

Listening Dictation ❖

Listen and fill in the blanks with the word you hear. Correct and discuss the dictation with your partner.

Most _____ schools will not accept young people who are _____ 17, have a history of school troubles, speak little _____ , or otherwise seem unlikely to be able ____ _____ the final exams and graduate in a reasonable amount of _____. ____ New York, a night _____ day school _____ created for these students.

Four_____ ago, just before his sixteenth _____, Jean-Luc Gerard landed at Kennedy _____ with $20.00 in his _____, alone, speaking no _____, and traumatized by the deaths of his uncle and brother in a West African civil war. _____ mother _____ kidnapped, and he _____ saw her again.

Four _____ later Mr. Gerard _____ graduated from this high school with a full _____ to Dartmouth College. He had been a night student while _____ full-time during the _____. The teachers helped _____ with tutoring. They _____ him English. They _____ him with immigration and gave him a mentor. The mentor even gave him a party when he was _____ to college.

More than half the students at the _____ are recent _____ like Mr. Gerard. Most come to school during the day for intensive _____ classes after they have been turned down by other high schools because of their age. No one at the school has much _____. Many students at the school hold some kind of _____ to support _____, their children, and sometimes other family _____.

Discussion ❖

Work with a partner. Share your ideas with the class.

1. What kind of future will Mr. Gerard have after he graduates from college?
2. What are some of the difficulties that he had to overcome in order to graduate from high school and receive a scholarship?
3. If you are an immigrant, what difficulties did you have to overcome, and still have to overcome?
4. Has anyone helped you? Who? Did it make a difference?

Writing ❖ *Choose **one** of the following topics.*

1. Write a paragraph about an opportunity you've had since you arrived in this country.

2. Do you have a lot of contact with others who came from your native country? In what ways do you help each other out?

3. Have you found what you were looking for in this country? Please explain.

Home Schooling

full text on page 140 (cd track 9)

Introduction ❖

Home schooling, the education of children at home by their parents or guardians, has gained in acceptance in the past 25 years. A recent estimate of the number of children in the United States who are schooled at home is approximately one million. The following is an interview with a parent who home-schooled her daughter, Eve, for five years. Eve will enter Michigan State University next September.

Vocabulary - (meanings limited to this context only) ❖

1. **challenge** - to test one's abilities; something that's difficult but not impossible
2. **conservative Christians** - people who want to include more religion in their children's education
3. **counterculture hippies** - young anti-government free thinkers
4. **approach** - a course of action
5. **virtual courses** - computer courses that seem like real life
6. **expertise** - a special skill in doing something
7. **network** - to meet and exchange information with people in similar situations
8. **isolated** - separated from others

Note Taking ❖

Listen and take notes. Do not try to write every word. When you are done, compare your notes with a partner. Did you get the important information?

Why did you choose home schooling for your daughter?

Is home schooling legal?

How does home schooling work?

Do you and your husband have teaching degrees?

Were you at all worried that Eve could become isolated from other people her age?

Discussion ❖ *With a partner, talk about these statements.*

A. Decide if these statements are Fact or Opinion.

( ) 1. Private schools are more expensive than public schools.

( ) 2. Private schools are better than public schools.

( ) 3. Home schooling is now legal in all 50 states.

( ) 4. Home schooling is better than the public schools.

( ) 5. Home schooling started back in the 1970s.

B. Decide if these statements are true or false -- or write IDK (I don't know)

( ) 1. Eve and her parents are very religious.

( ) 2. Eve was bored in public school.

( ) 3. Eve's parents both graduated from four-year universities.

( ) 4. Eve's mother does most of the teaching.

( ) 5. Eve received excellent grades in her courses.

( ) 6. Eve has opportunities to socialize with others her age.

( ) 7. You can't get accepted into a university if you have been schooled at home.

( ) 8. Home-schooled students are better prepared to enter a university than other students.

C. Talk about these questions with a partner. Share your ideas with the class.

1. According to Eve's mother, what are some advantages of home schooling?

2. What concerns do you have about home schooling?

3. What other questions would you have for Eve's parents?

4. More African-American and Latino parents are home schooling their children. Here are some of their complaints about public (and parochial) schools. Which do you agree/disagree with?

> overcrowded classrooms
>
> under-qualified teachers
>
> bullying by racists
>
> too much emphasis on passing state tests

Idioms ❖ *Discuss the meaning of these idioms and expressions with your class*

1. She's conservative. She's from the old school.
2. He's a socialist. He belongs to that school of thought.
3. He was schooled in the family business.
4. She's learning the ropes on her new job.
5. Sandra is the teacher's pet.
6. Bob's a smart aleck,- or a "know-it-all."
7. She knows her p's and q's.
8. She has the know-how to do her job well.

Writing ❖

From your notes, write a summary of the interview. You may take each question individually and respond in complete sentences or write a paragraph highlighting the important information.

A Success Story

full text on page 141 (cd track 10)

Introduction ❖

Donald Romano, a child of migrant workers, who spent his childhood working in the fields, had little opportunity for schooling but a great passion for learning. The following is an interview with Donald by a newspaper reporter.

Vocabulary ❖

1. **migrant worker** - an agricultural worker who picks fruits and vegetables and moves from area to area to do their job
2. **passion** - strong desire
3. **crops** - plants such as corn, wheat, rice, etc. that are grown by farmers
4. **modest** - shy, not talking about your achievements
5. **boredom** - not finding something interesting
6. **heavy heart** - great sadness
7. **MBA** - Master of Business Administration

Note Taking ❖

Listen to Donald's responses to these statements and questions and take notes. Do not try to write every word. When you are done, compare your notes with a partner.

Tell me about your family and your childhood.

What was your early schooling like?

I know that you did very well in high school. Can you tell us about it?

Some unfortunate things have happened to you, as well. Can you talk about these?

Please tell me about your university life and your plans for the future.

Discussion ❖ *With a partner, discuss the following questions. Share your ideas with the class.*

1. According to Donald, boredom was the thing that bothered him most when he worked in the fields. Can you understand this? Have you ever worked at a very boring job? Talk about it.

2. What is Donald's goal now that he has an MBA from Harvard? Does this surprise you?

3. Why did Donald find Harvard difficult at first? What was one cultural difference that he had to adjust to? Do you also find it difficult to speak up in the classroom?

4. How is he going to change his mother's life?

Writing ❖ *Choose one of the following and write a paragraph.*

Write a short summary of this interview. Use your notes to write it.

Write about a boring job that you have now or had in the past. Explain why it is boring.

Underage Drinking

full text on page 142 (cd track 11)

Introduction ❋

Here's a letter to an advice columnist about drinking and driving. Before you do the dictation, decide if the following statements are true or false. Discuss them with your classmates.

_____ The legal drinking age in this state is 21.

_____ The legal driving age in this state is 17.

_____ The cost of car insurance is higher for people under 25 years of age.

_____ In the U.S. motor vehicle accidents account for nearly 3/4 of all deaths among
       people aged 15-24.

Vocabulary ❋

1. **can't afford** - not able to pay for
2. **lend** - to allow someone to use for a period of time
3. **fanatic** - hysterical
4. **persuade** - to lead someone to believe or do

Paragraph Dictogloss ❋

Listen to the letter two or three times. First listening: listen only. Second listening: take notes or just listen again. Do not try to write every word. Third listening (if necessary): be sure to write something, even if it's only a few words.. When you are finished listening, try to write the main idea of the letter in one or two sentences. You can work with a partner. If necessary, your teacher will give you the paragraph again. Come to agreement with your class about the main idea of the letter. Share your ideas with the class and decide together what advice is best for George.

Dear Deena,

George from Georgetown

Role plays *

The class should be organized in groups of 3 or 4. Each group will create one of the scenes below and act it out for the class. Students have 10 minutes to create and practice. No writing is necessary. Decide what role you are going to play and what you are going to say as the scene develops. Each person should assume a role and a point of view. If you prefer not to assume a point of view, just present the discussion and the class will suggest a solution. Be sure you understand the problem!

1. **Scene one:** George wants to drive his parents' car and thinks it's okay to drive after only drinking two beers.

2. **Scene two**: Mary, age 21, a student, was arrested for driving drunk and has to pay $4000 for a lawyer, court costs, fines, and an alcohol education program. She tries to persuade her parents to help with the costs.

Writing * *Choose **one** of the following.*

1. Write a letter persuading a friend or parent to allow you to do something.

2. Write a paragraph responding to George.

Overprotected?

full text on page 143 (cd track 12)

Introduction ✳

Parents love their children. No matter how old they are, they worry about them and try very hard to keep them from away from danger. Some parents try too hard to protect their children. Were you overprotected when you were a child?

Vocabulary ✳

1. **overprotective** - so anxious to protect someone from harm that you restrict their freedom
2. **foreigner** - someone from a different country
3. **to pressure** - attempt to persuade someone by using influence, argument, or threat
4. **commute** - to travel from home to school or work and back
5. **prom** - a formal dance party for high school students
6. **on your own** - alone, by yourself
7. **instinct** - a natural tendency to behave or react in a particular way without having to learn about it or think about it

Prediction ✳ *This is a letter to an advice columnist. Work with a partner and decide on a word to fill in each blank space.*

Dear Amy,

I read you _____ the Internet because I _____ in Europe. I am _____ to a foreigner and _____ in his country. I love it here, but my problem is the difference in attitude about children. Specifically, I _____ a nine-year-old daughter who must take a bus to the train _____ and then a 20-minute _____ on a train to get to her school. It is a private bilingual _____. Many of the _____ in her _____ come from far _____ on their _____. In fact, this is quite common in their culture. Children are off to school on their _____ as young _____ kindergarten. My husband and my daughter's teacher have been pressuring me; she _____ I am overprotective, that I should let my daughter make this trip ____ _____. I am just _____ comfortable with this. I am American and my instinct is to not allow a nine-year-old to go through a big city train _____ on _____ _____. Am I overprotective? How can I ever _____ comfortable about this?

Kate

Listening Dictation ✳ *Listen and fill in the blanks with the word you hear. Then compare your prediction to the listening with a partner.*

Dear Amy,

I read you _____ the Internet because I _____ in Europe. I am _____ to a foreigner and _____ in his country. I love it here, but my problem is the difference in attitude about children. Specifically, I _____ a nine-year-old daughter who must take a bus to the train _____ and then a 20-minute _____ on a train to get to her school. It is a private bilingual _____. Many of the _____ in her _____ come from far _____ on their _____. In fact, this is quite common in their culture. Children are off to school on their _____ as young ____ kindergarten. My husband and my daughter's teacher have been pressuring me; she _____ I am overprotective, that I should let my daughter make this trip ___ _____. I am just _____ comfortable with this. I am American and my instinct is to not allow a nine-year-old to go through a big city train _____ on ____ _____. Am I overprotective? How can I ever _____ comfortable about this?

Kate

Discussion ❋ *Discuss these questions with a partner. Share your ideas with the class.*

1. Do you believe that Kate is being overprotective?
2. What do you think the mother is afraid of?
3. Are you now living in a country where children have more freedom than they do in your original country?

Discussion ❋ *Discuss the following situations.*

A. Your nine-year-old daughter's friend is having a "sleep-over" birthday party. The party begins with dinner at 6:00 p.m. and you are told to pick up your child at 10:00 the following morning. Do you let your child go?

B. High school seniors stay out all night on the night of the senior prom. The night begins with a dinner dance at a hotel, followed by a party at someone's house, and ends with breakfast at a popular restaurant. Your daughter really wants to go but your husband disapproves. What do you do?

C. Your three-year-old wants to climb to the top of a very big slide and then go down it herself. She screams when you try to help her. Do you let her do it alone?

Writing ❋ *Choose one of the following topics and write several paragraphs.*

1. Write a response to Kate giving her advice.
2. Write about the negative and/or positive effects of being overprotective.
3. Write about a time in your life when you were overprotective or a time when you were overprotected.

Driver's Licenses for Illegal Immigrants?

full text on page 144 (cd track 13)

Introduction ✳

According to the Immigration and Naturalization Service, legal immigration varies between 700,000 and 900,000 people each year. The agency also estimates that 420,000 illegal aliens enter the country every year. The total number of illegal aliens is about 7,000,000, most of whom are from Mexico. There is a lot of discussion about the rights and privileges of illegal immigrants. Here are some comments from Americans who were asked: "Should illegal immigrants be allowed to obtain driver's licenses?"

Vocabulary ✳

1. **privilege** - a benefit or special right given to a person
2. **criminal** - a person who commits a serious crime
3. **car insurance** - an agreement with an insurance company in which the company will pay for an accident in exchange for regular payments
4. **medical coverage** - medical insurance
5. **allowed** - permitted
6. **revoke** - cancel; take back a right or favor
7. **alien** - belonging to another country

Note taking ✳

The following six people were asked, "Should illegal immigrants be allowed to obtain driver's licenses?" Here are their responses. Listen and take notes. It is not necessary to write every word, only the information you think is important. When you are finished, go over your notes with a partner and discuss the dictation. What is your opinion? Give reasons.

1. Karen Johnson

2. Jason Garcia

3. Helen Chen

4. David Peterson

5. Susanne Roberts

6. Minnie Lee

Fact or Opinion? ✳

With a partner, decide if the statement is a FACT or OPINION. A fact is a generally accepted true statement, whereas an opinion expresses a personal feeling or point of view. Write O for opinion and F for fact. Share your answers with the class.

( ) 1. There are too many immigrants in the United States.

( ) 2. 75% of illegal immigrants come from Mexico.

( ) 3. The U.S. government is not doing enough to help immigrants.

( ) 4. The U.S. government shouldn't try to help illegal immigrants.

( ) 5. The U.S. government deports only 1% of illegal aliens.

Discussion   ✳ *With a partner, talk about these issues.*

_____ 1. Two years ago, Wal-Mart, a large company that has 3500 stores in the U.S., got into trouble for hiring illegal immigrants to clean their stores at night. If a company knows it is hiring illegal immigrants, it may go to court and face criminal and civil penalties. How can companies know if a person is legal or not?

_____ 2. Nine of the 250 illegal immigrants who were arrested have decided to sue Wal-Mart. They said they were paid lower salaries and were offered fewer benefits because they are Mexicans. They say they were paid $350 to $500 a week and did not get overtime pay. This is the first time illegal aliens have sued. Do you think they have a chance of winning?

_____ 3. The U.S. government is offering $1 billion to hospitals that provide emergency care to illegal aliens. For years, hospitals said that the U.S. government was responsible for immigration policy and should pay for the costs of illegal immigrants because it had created the problem. Hospital employees, however, see problems because the government wants them to ask patients questions such as (1) "Are you a legal immigrant with a valid green card?" and (2) "What kind of visa do you have?" What problems do you think these questions can cause?

_____ 4. Lawmakers in one state want to allow 400 children of illegal aliens to qualify for in-state tuition at local state colleges and universities. Lawmakers argue that it is not right to punish students who might have been brought here illegally when they were children. This would apply only to students who have lived in the state for three years, graduated from a high school in that state, and filed an affidavit saying they were beginning the process of becoming citizens. Is this a good idea?

Writing ✳

Use your notes from the note-taking activity to summarize why illegal immigrants should or should not be allowed to obtain driver's licenses.

Dear Mom and Dad

Introduction ✳

full text on page 145 (cd track 14)

Have you ever tried to prepare someone for bad news rather than telling them the bad news directly? This is what a college student tries to do in this letter to her parents.

Vocabulary ✳

1. **thoughtless** - not caring, not considerate
2. **up to date** - to this point, so far, up to now
3. **I am getting along** - I am doing well
4. **skull** - bony framework of the head
5. **fracture** - a break, particularly of a bone
6. **concussion** - injury to the brain caused by a hard blow
7. **dormitory** - college housing
8. **open arms** - a warm, welcoming reception
9. **tolerance** - acceptance

Dictation ✳

In the first part of the letter fill in the blanks with the words you hear. In the second part of the letter put in the correct tense of the verb that is given . Correct and discuss the letter with a partner.

Dear Mom and Dad,

Since I left for college, I _____ _____ very bad about writing, and I am sorry for my thoughtlessness in not _____ written before. I will bring you up to date now, but before you read on, please sit down. You are not to read any further unless you are sitting down. Okay?

Well then, I am getting along pretty well now. The skull fracture and the concussion I got when I _____ out of the window of my dormitory when it _____ on fire is pretty well _____ now. I only _____ two weeks in the hospital, and now I can see almost normally and only _____ these sick headaches once a day. Fortunately, the fire in my dormitory and my jump _____ _____ by an attendant at the gas station near the dorm, and he was the one who _____ the fire department and the ambulance. He also _____ me in the hospital, _____ ____ flowers, and since then we _____ _____ in love. We are _____ ____ marry, and I ____ _____ the university in order to find a job. He is _____ and has three young children that he _____ _____ . This is difficult ____ ____ on a gas station attendant's salary, and I _____ _____ .

Pairwork ✳ *The letter continues. With a partner, decide what form of the verb goes in each blank. The first two are done for you*

I ___*know*___ (to know) that you ___*will welcome*___ (to welcome) him into our family with

open arms. He _____ (to be) kind, and although not well educated he _____ (to be) ambi-

tious. Although he _____ (to be) of a different race and religion than ours, I know you will

not be _____ (to bother) by that.

   Now that I _____ _____ (to bring) you up to date, I want to tell you that there

_____ (to be) no dormitory fire. I _____ _____ _____ (to not have) a concussion or skull

fracture. I _____ _____ (to not be) in the hospital and there _____ (to be) no boyfriend in

my life. However, I am _____ (to get) a D in history and F in science, and I _____

(to want) you to see those marks in their proper perspective.

                              Your loving daughter,

                              Susan

Discussion   ✳ *Discuss these questions wth a partner. Share your answers and ideas with the class.*

1. Did the ending surprise you?
2. Do you think that Susan's parents put the "D" and the "F" in their proper perspective?
3. Can you think of an occasion when you prepared someone for the hard truth that you had to tell them?

Writing   ✳ *Choose **one** of the following topics to write about.*

1. Write a letter to Susan from her mother and father in response to her letter.

2. There are many reasons for poor grades. List as many as you can, but a minimum of five.

    1. I didn't study for the test.

    2.

    3.

    4.

    5.

Bad Dog? Bad Owner?

full text on page 146 (cd track 15)

Introduction ❋

We often hear dog owners say, "Bad dog!" when the new puppy has just chewed up a shoe. But how often do we hear someone say "Bad owner!" when the dog's owner has allowed his dog to dig in someone's garden?

Vocabulary ❋

1. **puppy** - a young dog
2. **chew** - to bite food several times before swallowing it
3. **selectman** - an elected member of a town government
4. **vicious** - violent and dangerous
5. **tolerate** - to accept something bad or different without criticizing it
6. **DNA** - an acid that carries genetic information in a cell
7. **convict** - to prove that someone is guilty of a crime
8. **dental retainer** - something worn over teeth to help make them straight
9. **misbehave** - to act badly and cause trouble or annoy people

Dictation ❋ *Listen and write the words you hear. Correct and discuss with a partner.*

1. In a small town on Martha's Vineyard in Massachusetts, the town selectmen _____ ____ _____ a decision about Sabrina, a large dog _____ _____ _____ and eaten several chickens belonging to a neighbor. "I don't think we should be tolerating this," said _____ ____ _____ selectmen. "_____ _____ some chickens to dogs myself, and I think a vicious dog _____ _____ _____ should be destroyed." What was unusual about this situation was that the owner ____ _____ _____ found dog hairs in the chicken house. He took hairs from three of his neighbors' dogs _____ _____ _____ to a DNA lab. Sabrina's was a _____ _____ The woman in the lab said that this was the first time _____ _____ _____ convict a four-legged killer.

What do you think should be done to the dog?

What do you think should be done to Sabrina's owner?

2. Mrs. Minami lives in a pretty house with a garden that she ____ _____ ____. Her next-door neighbor, Mr. Sampson, has a twelve-year-old son, Ralph, _____ _____ ___ _____ named Storm. He often lets Storm _____ ___ _____ _____ on her own. Storm likes to go into Mrs. Minami's garden and _____ _____ and _____ _____. Mrs. Minami _____ _____ twice to Mr. Sampson and to Ralph, but _____ _____ _____.

What should Mrs. Minami do now?

3. Jeffrey had agreed_____ _____ Buffy, a poodle, for a weekend because his good friends, the Cogans, were going to a family wedding. After _____ _____ _____, and Buffy had gone home, Jeffrey's wife found their eleven-year-old's _____ _____ dental retainer on the floor _____ ___ _____ _____ in it. It will cost approximately $500.00 ____ _____.

Who should be responsible for paying for the dental retainer?

Discussion   ✳ *Discuss these questions with a partner. Share your ideas with the class.*

1. Do you own a pet? Have you ever owned a pet? Has your pet ever "misbehaved"? Tell your partner what happened.
2. Have you ever had a bad experience with an animal? Talk about it.
3. If a dog bites a human, do you think the dog should be killed?

Idioms   ✳   *Here are some common idioms. Can you and your partner guess what they mean?*

His bark is worse than his bite.
It's a dog-eat-dog world.
I don't enjoy the dog days of August.
Because he forgot her birthday, he's in the doghouse.
She asked the waiter to put the rest of her dinner in a doggy bag.
He leads a dog's life.
This country is really going to the dogs.
Let sleeping dogs lie.

Writing ✳ *Choose one of the following topics.*

1. If you own a pet, list your responsibilities to your pet, and then list your responsibilities to your community.

Responsibilities to Pet

Responsibilities to Community

2. Write about a pet you love or a pet you loved in the past.

Bullies

full text on page 147 (cd track 16)

Introduction ✳

In every class there seems to be a bully, a boy or girl who threatens or even hits other students in their class. This is not just a problem in the United States. Bullies are everywhere. Before you begin the dictation, talk about a bully you know or have heard of.

Vocabulary ✳

1. **pick on** - to decide to bother or hurt someone; to tease
2. **punish** - to make someone pay for doing something wrong; to discipline
3. **menial** - boring, unpleasant, lowly
4. **chores** - boring but necessary acts/tasks
5. **incident** - a happening; usually a bad event
6. **suicide** - the act of killing oneself; taking one's own life
7. **make fun of** - to pick on someone; to tease or ridicule
8. **shove** - a hard push with the hands
9. **pull off** - to pull hard and remove
10. **insurance** - an agreement with a company in which the company will pay for a loss or damage
11. **siempre** - A Spanish word meaning always

Dictation ✳

Listen and fill in the blanks. Correct and discuss solutions to these problems with a partner.

Case One. Elementary School

Billy was a _____-_____-_____fifth grader who was _____ _____ from school one day. In front of him were _____ _____ _____. Billy began picking on them, so the girls _____ _____ to their teacher the next day. The teacher then punished Billy by having him _____ _____ _____ and clean the boards and perform other menial chores. Billy's parents _____ _____ _____ the punishment. They felt that because the incident happened after school, it was not _____ _____ _____.

Do you think the teacher was correct in punishing Billy? Explain why or why not.

Case Two. Middle School

Rosie goes to a program ____ _____ _____ called ROPES, which stands for "Respect Other

People Equally Siempre." The program ____ _____ ____ help stop bullying, but Rosie

still has problems with one girl, Linda, who picks on her for____ _____ _____.

Lately, Linda has been teasing her _____ _____. She is hurt by the bad names she calls her,

and the situation is getting so bad that she ____ _____ ____ suicide. Her friends say

that Linda bullies her because _____ _____ _____ _____, but Rosie sees

no reason for Linda to make fun of her.

What can Rosie do to stop Linda from bullying her?

Case Three. High School

Robert _____ _____ ___ _____ in school with another boy named Charles. Charles

started the fight and was often teasing and shoving Robert ____ _____ _____. Dur-

ing the fight, Charles pulled off Robert's _____ _____ and kept it. He refused to return

it. Robert ____ _____ ____ complain to his teacher because he _____ _____

_____ _____ _____.

What do you think Robert should do?

Have you ever heard of bully insurance? (The French have it.) What services can

it offer people, do you think?

Discussion ✳ *With the class, discuss the following statements.*

1. Parents should let children fight their own battles.
2. Most bullies come from unhappy families.
3. Children who are bullied will have problems later in life.
4. Teachers should call parents and tell them that their child is bullying other students.
5. Bullies are born, not made.

Writing ✳ *Choose **one** of the two items below.*

1. Choose one of the statements in the discussion section above and write a paragraph about your opinion.

2. Write about an experience that you had that involved bullying (about a situation when you were bullied or when you bullied someone else).

How Honest Are You? *full text on page 148 (cd track 17)*

Introduction ❋

If you lose a $100 bill on the street in most major cities in the world, would you expect someone to return it to a police station or a lost and found department?

Vocabulary ❋

1. **to claim** - prove that it's yours and have it returned to you
2. **metropolitan area** - city
3. **hand in** - give to somebody in authority
4. **from early on** - from when you are young

Pair Dictation   ❋ *In the dictation here and on the next page, work in pairs and dictate to each other. Student A has half of the dictation and reads their lines to Student B, who has the other half (A dictates and B writes). Then Student B dictates and A writes until the dictation is complete. When you are finished, check your completed dictation with your partner.*

❋ Student A ❋

_____ ____ an article in the New York Times ____ _____ ___, _____,

titled "Never Lost but Found Daily: Japanese Honesty," ___ _____ _____ a $100 bill ____

_____, there is a good chance _____ ____ _____ ___ _____, and you could

claim it.

____ _____, with eight million people ____ _____ _____, and thirty-three million

___ _____ _____ _____, a $100 bill _____ _____ _____

_____ _____ to the Tokyo Metropolitan Police _____ _____ _____ _____.

In 2002, _____ _____ _____ _____ to the Tokyo Center _____-

_____ _____ in cash. 72% of it was returned ____ _____ _____ once they had

persuaded the police ___ ____ _____. About _____ went to the finders _____

___ _____ claimed the money _____ _____ ___ _____.

Children are taught _____ _____ ____ to hand in anything they find ____ ____

_____ in their neighborhood.

___ _____ _____ _____ _____ is umbrellas, _____ ___ _____.

The item _____ ____ _____ _____ ___ _____ is the cell phone, 75%.

Do people in your city return things they find? ____ _____?

Pair Dictation   ✳   *In the dictation here and on page 51, work in pairs and dictate to each other. Student A has half of the dictation and reads their lines to Student B, who has the other half (A dictates and B writes). Then Student B dictates and A writes until the dictation is complete. When you are finished, check your completed dictation with your partner.*

✳ Student B ✳

According to ____ _____ ____ _____ _____ _____ _____ on January 8, 2004,

_____ _____ _____ _____ _____ _____: _____ _____,

if you lost ____ _____ _____ in Tokyo, _____ ___ ___ _____ _____ that it would

be returned, _____ _____ _____ _____ ___.

In Tokyo, _____ ___ _____ _____ in the city, _____ _____-

_____ _____ in the metropolitan area, _____ _____ _____ would probably find

its way ____ _____ _____ _____ _____ Lost and Found Center.

____ _____, people found and brought ____ _____ _____ _____ twenty-three

million ___ _____. _____ ___ ___ _____ _____ to the owners _____

_____ _____ _____ _____ _____ it was theirs. _____ 19% _____

___ _____ _____ after no one _____ _____ _____ for half a year.

_____ _____ _____ from early on ___ _____ ___ _____ _____

_____ to the police ____ _____ _____.

The most frequently lost item ___ _____, 360,000 in 2002. _____ _____ with

the highest rate of return ___ _____ _____ _____, _____.

____ _____ ___ _____ _____ _____ _____ _____ _____?

Do you ?

Discussion   ✳   *Work with a partner and discuss these questions.*

1. Have you ever found anything? What did you do with it? Have you ever lost anything? What happened?

2. Do you think that if you live in an honest society, you are a more honest person, and that if you live in a dishonest society, you will probably be more dishonest?

3. Are you more honest if a small store owner would be hurt than if a large company or the government would be hurt? For example, would you return $10 to a small store owner if he gave you too much change by mistake? Would you return it to a large store like WalMart?

Discussion ✳

Discuss the following three situations with your partner and tell what you would do in each situation.

1. You've just checked into a hotel room and discovered an expensive watch near the phone. Would you call the hotel management and tell them about the watch?

2. When withdrawing money from an ATM, you receive an extra $200.00. Your account, however, doesn't show this. Would you keep the money?

3. The government has given you a large tax refund by mistake. Do you tell them?

Writing ✳ *Sometimes it is better to lie than tell the truth. Do you agree or disagree?*

Subway Manners

full text on page 148 (cd track 18)

Introduction ✳

How do you get to work or school? Do you drive or use public transportation? What do you like about public transportation and what don't you like about it?

Vocabulary ✳
1. **etiquette** - manners; forms of conduct for polite society
2. **personal space** - the amount of space that belongs to you; not getting too close to another person
3. **annoying** - making one feel slightly angry
4. **irritating** - making one feel slightly angry
5. **off-putting** - making one feel disgusted
6. **electronic devices** - cell phones, hand-held games, palm pilots
7. **senior citizens** - people over the age of 65
8. **gossip** - conversation about other people's behavior and private lives
9. **starved** - very hungry
10. **backpack** - a bag carried on one's back

Dictation ✳

Here are a few basic etiquette rules that will help you and all those around you during your train ride.

1. When reading your newspaper, keep it _____ your own personal space. Don't block another's personal space. Take your paper with you when you leave the train . _____ _____ ____ _____ on the seat.

2. Please don't let _____ _____ _____ ring, or worse yet, play ___ _____ _____ _____. Research indicates that one of the _____ _____ _____ is being forced to listen to someone's one-sided cell phone conversation.

3. Avoid eating _____, _____, or _____ food on a train. The _____, _____, and _____ are off-putting to those around you.

4. Avoid computer or gaming sounds on your electronic devices. Again, noises are irritating to _____ _____.

5. If you must _____ ____ _____, lower your head and cover your mouth with a tissue to avoid spreading your germs to those _____ _____.

6. Help passengers who may need help ____ ____ _____ the train, and _____ _____ _____ to a senior citizen or pregnant woman.

7. Avoid staring ____ _____ _____. You may not even be conscious of staring.

Discussion   ✳ *Consider the following situations with a partner. How would you respond to each one?*

1. You are a young man and tired after a long day of work. A woman gets on the train and stands in front of you. Do you offer her your seat?

2. You are on a crowded train. Suddenly the cell phone in your backpack rings. It is your best friend calling. Do you begin a long gossipy conversation?

3. You get on the train and you are starved. Do you take out a tuna fish sandwich from your lunch bag and begin to eat?

4. There is a fascinating woman sitting across from you. She wears ten earrings in one ear, she has several tattoos, and her hair is dyed purple. Would you stare at her?

5. The train stops between stations. Five minutes later it still has not moved. The conductor has not made any announcements. Would you begin to complain loudly?

Writing   ✳ *Choose **one** of the following topics.*

1. What is one of the best or worst experiences you've had on a bus, subway, or train?

2. Compare public transportation in a city you have lived in with transportation in the city you are living in now.

✤ AMERICANA ✤

Rights and Responsibilities of Citizenship

full text on page 149 (cd track 19)

Introduction ✤

After you have been in the United States legally for five years, you can become a citizen. Then you will have the same rights and responsibilities as other Americans. Before you begin, talk about how different modal auxiliaries can change the meaning of a sentence.

Lulu _____ take the citizenship test.

a. must   **b.** could   **c.** should   **d.** ought to   **e.** will   **f.** is supposed to   **g.** will be able to   **h.** can

Vocabulary ✤

1. **right** - ability to do something guaranteed by law
2. **responsibility** - an obligation or duty; something you must do because of a moral/legal necessity
3. **vote** - to choose
4. **election** - an event when people vote for or against someone
5. **volunteer** - to agree to do something (by choice) at no cost to anyone
6. **jury duty** - the obligation to sit in a court, listen to a trial, and decide guilt or innocence
7. **show up** - to arrive
8. **run for office** - to try to get elected
9. **armed forces** - the military (Army, Navy, Marines, etc.)
10. **well-informed** - having a lot of information

Dictation ❖

Listen and fill in the blanks with the words you hear. Then correct and discuss with a partner. Decide together if the statement is a right (rt) or a responsibility (rs) of citizenship.

Here are two examples to be sure you understand the task.

____Rt____ 1. You can have a U.S. passport.

____Rs____ 2. You must obey the laws.

_____ 1. You _____ ____ _____ ____ vote in national, state, and local elections.

_____ 2. If you want, you _____ _____ _____ political office or hold a government job.

_____ 3. You _____ _____ in all elections.

_____ 4. You _____ _____ ____ show up for jury duty.

_____ 5. You _____ _____ to serve in the armed forces.

_____ 6. If you work, you _____ _____ ____ pay federal income taxes.

_____ 7. You _____ ____ become a well-informed citizen by reading the newspaper.

Fact or Opinion? ❖

With a partner, decide if the statement is FACT or OPINION. A fact is a generally accepted statement of truth that you can check in a dictionary, encyclopedia, or other reference source. An opinion, on the other hand, expresses a personal feeling, idea, or point of view. Write F for Fact and O for Opinion. Share your answers with the class.

____1. George Washington was the first president.

____2. George Washington was the best president.

____3. Democracy is the best form of government.

____4. The right to vote is generally considered to be the most important right of citizenship.

Discussion ❖ Cooperative learning activity

Work in groups with 3, 4, or 5 students in each group. Each student finds the answers to one or several questions and reports back to their group. Then all four groups share the answers they have found in reconfigured groups, each person responsible for all of the answers from their group.

Group One

1. Who elects the President of the U.S.?
2. How many stars are there on the American flag? Why?
3. What is the basic belief of the Declaration of Independence?
4. Which president was the first Commander in Chief of the U.S. military?
5. What is the Constitution?

Group Two

1. What are the two major political parties?
2. Who helped the Pilgrims in America?
3. Which president freed the slaves?
4. How many terms can the president serve?
5. What is the Congress?

Group Three

1. Who was the president during the Civil War?
2. What is the capital of your state and who is its governor?
3. What is the minimum voting age?
4. What are the three branches of government?
5. Name one purpose of the United Nations.

Group Four

1. What is the title of the national anthem?
2. Name one benefit of being a citizen of the U.S.
3. What country did the American colonies fight during the Revolutionary War?
4. What are the 49th and 50th states of the union?
5. What is the Bill of Rights?

Writing ❖

On your computer, type in "U.S. Citizenship Exam" and do a search for the 100 questions on the exam. Write down five questions that you want to ask the class tomorrow. Do you know the answers? Include at least one question about the Constitution and the Bill of Rights, a good way to practice your modals.

Non-English Speakers in the U.S.

full text on page 149 (cd track 20)

Introduction ✧

Because of the increase in immigration since 1990, America has become a multi-lingual nation. Many school districts are looking for bilingual teachers to teach immigrant students. America Online now offers an AOL Latino service. It reaches homes where Spanish is the dominant language. Census Bureau questionnaires were printed in Spanish, Chinese, Vietnamese, and Korean. Many companies now have advertising and marketing campaigns to reach people who speak languages other than English. What language or languages do you speak at home? What languages do the people you live with speak?

Vocabulary ✧

1. **dominant** - stronger; more important
2. **over the age of** - older than
3. **other than** - besides
4. **to surge** - to increase suddenly
5. **bilingual** - speaking two languages
6. **bilingual education** - students learn in first and second languages in school
7. **Census Bureau** - the government office that counts people

Dictogloss ✧

Listen to a complete sentence only once and write down the words you can remember on a separate piece of paper. With a partner, try to reconstruct the entire sentence and write it below.

1.

2.

3.

4.

5.

Discussion ❖ *Discuss these questions with a partner. Share your ideas with the class.*

1. At home, do you listen to any programs that are not in English? Which ones?
Do you read an English language newspaper or magazine? If not, which ones
do you read?

2. What do you think are the advantages and disadvantages of bilingual education?

Writing ❖ *Write about your best or your worst experience speaking English.*

Yard Sales

Introduction ✧

full text on page 150 (cd track 21)

Concerned about frugal living and saving money? Ready to move and need to clean out your house? Just need to clear out the clutter? Join 60 million people who go to yard or garage sales every year.

Vocabulary ✧

1. **yard sale** - informal selling of things no longer wanted, usually held in a yard or garage
2. **frugal** - careful about spending money
3. **clutter** - useless stuff that occupies space
4. **pack rat** - a person who keeps collecting things and never throws anything away
5. **reread** - to read for a second time
6. **to be addicted to** - must do, cannot do without

Prediction Dictation ✧

In this dictation you are not going to listen first. Work with a partner and fill in each blank with the word you think is correct. When you are finished, you will listen and do the dictation on the next page. Then compare your responses.

Carol and Alan _____ _____ married _____ 25 years. It is a good marriage and they _____ happy. _____ there is one problem; Alan is a pack rat. He _____ throws anything away. He _____ two newspapers every day and keeps most of them around the house in case he wants to reread an article. Most of the _____ he never does.

He is also addicted to yard _____, and almost every weekend he comes _____ with several things. For instance, he often _____ toys for a day in the future when he has a grandchild. He also _____ broken chairs that he plans to _____ one day in the _____. He never _____ anything out. The house is becoming more and _____ crowded with things that are never used.

Carol, on the other _____, throws _____ anything she is sure she will never use again. When Alan is _____ of the house, she _____ away lots of newspapers and some other_____.

Once when he asked where something she had thrown _____ was, she _____, "I have no idea where it can be."

Listening Dictation ❖ *Fill in the blanks with the word or words you hear. Then, with a partner, check your dictation and discuss it.*

Carol and Alan _____ _____ married _____ 25 years. It is a good marriage and they _____

happy. _____ there is one problem. Alan is a pack rat. He _____ throws anything away. He

_____ two newspapers every day and keeps most of them around the house in case he wants

to reread an article. Most of the _____ he never does.

He is also addicted to yard _____, and almost every weekend he comes _____ with several

things. For instance, he often _____ toys for a day in the future when he has a grandchild. He also

_____ broken chairs that he plans to _____ one day in the _____. He never _____

anything out. The house is becoming more and _____ crowded with things that are never used.

Carol, on the other _____, throws _____ anything she is sure she will never use again. When

Alan is_____of the house, she _____ away lots of newspapers and some other_____.

Once when he asked where something that she had thrown _____ was, she _____, "I

have no idea where it can be."

Discussion ❖ *Discuss these questions with a partner, Share your ideas with the class.*

1. Have you ever had a yard sale? What are some of the things you sold?

2. Have you ever been to a yard sale? What are some of the things you bought?

3. Do you ever throw out things that you know you will never use again? Do you keep these things?

4. Do you sympathize with Carol, who throws things out but doesn't tell her husband?

5. Andrea and Alfonso are a young couple who have just married . They have rented a small apartment but have nothing to put in it. American friends have told them about yard sales and one Saturday morning they go to look for things. They have $200.00 to spend. With a partner, decide how they might spend their money. Here are some of the things they found at the yard sale.

1. a pretty bedspread $3.00
2. a sofa bed $50.00
3. a comfortable chair, good condition $40.00
4. a comfortable chair, poor condition $20.00
5. a coffee table $20.00
6. a table lamp which needs a shade $10.00
7. 5 forks $1.50
8. a stroller $10.00
9. a spice rack $3.00
10. a bureau with four large drawers $15.00
11. a bunch of hangers $0.50
12. a toaster oven $2.00
13. a skillet $2.00
14. a blue parka $8.00
15. hardcover books $1.00 each
16. small blue rug $5.00
17. small plants $0.50 each
18. a small unit with radio, tape and CD player $15.00
19. a bath mat $3.00
20. a kitchen table with 3 chairs $50.00
21. a kettle $2.00
22. a standing lamp $20.00
23. 3 mugs $1.00
24. 4 knives $1.50
25. a hamper $4.00
26. 7 tablespoons $1.50
27. a box of toy cars $5.00
28. a large pot $2.00
29. 2 old telephones $5.00
30. 19-inch television $25.00
31. paperback books 50 cents each
32. a beautiful picture in a frame $5.00

Writing ✤ *Write a paragraph explaining some of the reasons you made the above choices for Andrea and Alfonso.*

.

Amy Tan, Writer

full text on page 151 (cd track 22)

Introduction ✤

Amy Tan is known for her best-selling book, *The Joy Luck Club*. She was born in California to parents who immigrated from China to escape the Chinese Civil War. Her novels center around the cultural norms and conflicts of Chinese-American families. *The Joy Luck Club* has been translated into 17 languages and was made into a movie.

Work with a partner and read the sentences, which outline a short biography of Amy Tan. Put them in chronological or logical order.

____ 1. In 1987, at age 35, Amy first visited China with her elderly mother. The trip changed her life.

____ 2. When she was a child, Amy's parents expected her to become a doctor and a concert pianist.

____ 3. After receiving her bachelor's and master's degrees from San Jose State, she enrolled in a doctoral program at UC Berkeley.

____ 4. Amy's mother enrolled her in a Baptist college in CA to study pre-med but Amy rebelled and followed her boyfriend to San Jose State University, where she studied English and linguistics.

____ 5. Amy was born in Oakland, California, in 1952.

____ 6. When Amy's father and brother both died of brain tumors within a year, Amy and her mother and her other brother moved to Switzerland, where Amy finished high school.

____ 7. In 1974, Amy married Louis DeMattei, an attorney who practiced tax law.

____ 8. Today, Ms. Tan continues to write not only novels but also children's books.

____ 9. The trip allowed Amy to see where her mother's roots came from and was the inspiration for Amy to complete stories she had started writing at home.

Vocabulary ✤
1. **rebel** - to fight against another person or group in power
2. **roots** - family connections in a place and through time
3. **conflicted** - unable to choose
4. **realize** - to understand, start to believe something is true
5. **identity** - who someone is or what someone is; a sense of oneself
6. **get along with** - to have a friendly relationship with

Dictation ❖

Here is part of an interview with Amy Tan. In this interview she was asked what advice she had either for children of bi-cultural parents or for first-generation children whose parents were born in another country. Here is her response. Correct and discuss the dictation with a partner.

First, I would say to them, you _____ _____ _____. I thought I was (in the 50s and 60s), and I _____ _____ ____ until I wrote *The Joy Luck Club*. I had so many readers who said, "I feel as though you've _____ ___ _____." A lot of young people come up to me and say, "I feel the same way, and I still feel that way. I don't get along with my mother and I'm the only kid in an _____- _____ _____ . And I don't know ___ ___ _____. Am I American? Am I Korean? What should I be? How should I feel about this?"

It's _____ ___ _____, but this feeling changes over time. It's normal to _____ _____. What you'll find later on is that _____ _____ _____ of who you are is a very, very interesting question, and having two cultures to add ___ _____ _____ of it makes it even more interesting. If you ever have a chance ___ ___ _____ to the country of your parents or your ancestors, you'll find out, not how Chinese or Korean or Indian you are, you'll find out _____ _____ _____ _____. This will give you a sense of perspective and humor that will help you find your own identity.

Discussion ❖ *Work with a partner and discuss these questions. Share your answers with the class.*

1. As a teenager, Amy rebelled against her parents and started dating a man, 24, who was 8 years older. She says, "Anything that my mother hated, I tried." What are some other ways teenagers rebel against their parents?

2. Amy won an essay contest when she was eight years old. The title of the essay was "What the Library Means to Me." She says, "The library published my essay and gave me a transistor radio, and at that moment, there was a little gleam in my mind that maybe I could earn money from writing." When you were in elementary school did you have any idea of what you wanted to be when you grew up? Has that changed? How? Was salary important?

Writing ❖

Ms. Tan says that it took her a long time to learn how to write the stories that ended up being The Joy Luck Club. *She says, "At first, I wanted to write stories for myself and become good at it. Writing was very private. But those first stories were not from my own experiences. I made up things that were completely alien to my life. It took me a while to realize that you need to write about the things you know from your own experiences."*

Option 1.   Write about a person who has influenced you in your life. This might be a parent or other family member, a friend, or a teacher. Explain how this person helped you in some way.

Option 2.   Write a short biography of a parent or friend who was born in another country.

For a more complete interview with Amy Tan, log on to:

http://www.achievement.org/autodoc/page/tan0int–1

Thanksgiving

full text on page 152 (cd track 23)

Introduction ❖

Thanksgiving is a national holiday that is celebrated by all Americans. It is a time for families and friends to get together and give thanks for the good things in life. It was the first holiday celebrated by American colonists.

Before you begin, tell the class what you know about Thanksgiving.

Vocabulary ❖
1. **pumpkin** - a large orange vegetable with a hard outside shell and soft insides with seeds
2. **tasty** - flavorful; yummy (slang)
3. **Pilgrims** - people who first came from Europe to the New World
4. **religious** - having strong beliefs in religion
5. **Indians** - people who are related to any of the original people of America; Native Americans
6. **celebrate** - to do something special (like having a party) for a special event
7. **crowded** - full of people

Dictation ❖

Listen and fill in the blanks. With a partner, decide if the statement is FACT or OPINION. A fact is a generally accepted statement of truth that you can check in a dictionary, encyclopedia, or other reference source. An opinion, on the other hand, expresses a personal feeling, idea, or point of view. Write F for Fact and O for Opinion. Share your answers with the class.

____1. Thanksgiving always comes on the _____ _____ in November.

____2. It is the _____ _____ American holiday.

____3. Many people have a big dinner that includes _____ and _____ _____ .

____4. Turkey is tastier _____ _____ .

____5. Thanksgiving dinners are ____ _____ ___ _____ to prepare.

____6. The Pilgrims started this tradition of _____ _____ in 1621.

____7. They came to Plymouth, Massachusetts, in 1620 to find_____ _____

.

____8. They came ____ _____ _____ and didn't have enough food to eat.

____9. _____ _____ helped them by giving them food and showing them how ____

_____ .

___10. At the end of their first year in America, the Pilgrims _____ _____ Indians to celebrate with a _____ _____ in appreciation for their help in surviving their first year.

___11. Thanksgiving is _____ _____ travel holiday of the year. Airports are _____ .

Discussion ❖ *Discuss another holiday with a partner. Include the following facts and opinions:*

1. The name of the holiday is _____ .

2. It is a _____ holiday. (national, religious, children's)

3. We celebrate this holiday on _____. (date(s))

4. We have been celebrating this holiday for _____ years.

5. On this holiday, everyone _____, _____, and _____.
   (Talk about food, clothing, other customs)

6. This holiday is important because _____ .

7. I like it because _____ .

Writing ❖

 Write a paragraph about a holiday or special day that is important to you. Use the points discussed above to guide you. Remember that there are different kinds of holidays or special events such as Mother's Day, Teacher's Day, and Children's Day.

A Tour of Washington, D.C.

full text on page 153 (cd track 24)

Introduction ✛

Have you ever gone on a tour when you were on vacation? Here is a tour guide leading a group around Washington, D.C., the capital of the United States.

> ## Vocabulary ✛
> **1. start off with a bang -** begin with something fun and exciting
> **2. a hop, skip, and a jump -** nearby

Prediction Dictation ✛

In this dictation you are not going to listen first. Work with a partner and fill in each blank with a word you think is correct. When you are finished, you will listen to the dictation on the next page. Then compare your responses.

Good morning, ladies and _____ , boys and _____. My name is George, and I am

your personal tour guide. For the_____ six hours, we _____ be exploring exciting Washington,

D.C., the _____ of the United States. Let's start off with a bang and visit the _____

House, D.C.'s _____ popular tourist attraction. Who knows, _____we'll even get to _____

the president at work in the Oval Office. Then it's only a hop, skip, and a jump to the Smithsonian

Institute where you _____ probably spend a whole week, there's so much to _____.   Then it's

on to the Lincoln Memorial. If you ask 100 Americans who the greatest _____ of the U.S.

was, most will say Abraham Lincoln. That's because he signed the Emancipation Proclamation to free

the slaves. And here's the Big One! For lunch, we're _____ to the Capitol Building Cafeteria,

where you'll get to _____ famous politicians like Senator Ted Kennedy. You may even ask them to

sign their autographs for the low, low, low price of $50. HA! HA! HA! All aboard!

Listening Dictation ✧ *Listen and fill in the blanks with the word you hear. Then compare your prediction to the listening with a partner.*

Good morning, ladies and _____, boys and _____. My name is George, and I am

your personal tour guide. For the_____ six hours, we _____ be exploring exciting Washington,

D.C., the _____ of the United States. Let's start off with a bang and visit the _____

House, D.C.'s _____ popular tourist attraction. Who knows, _____we'll even get to _____

the president at work in the Oval Office. Then it's only a hop, skip, and a jump to the Smithsonian

Institute where you _____ probably spend a whole week, there's so much to _____. Then it's

on to the Lincoln Memorial. If you ask 100 Americans who the greatest _____ of the U.S.

was, most will say Abraham Lincoln. That's because he signed the Emancipation Proclamation to free

the slaves. And here's the Big One! For lunch, we're _____ to the Capitol Building Cafeteria,

where you'll get to _____ famous politicians like Senator Ted Kennedy. You may even ask them to

sign their autographs for the low, low, low price of $50. HA! HA! HA! All aboard!

Discussion ✛ *With a partner, discuss the following items. Share your answers with the class.*

1. Have you ever been to Washington, D.C.? If so, tell the class about it.

2. Tell your group about the best (or worst) vacation you have ever had.

3. Make a list of the main tourist attractions in a city you know, or the city you are living in now. Tell your group why everyone should see these places when they visit.

4. You are visiting a famous place, like Hollywood, CA, and you only have three hours, so you decide to take a bus tour. What are some advantages and disadvantages of taking a bus tour?

Writing ✛ *After discussing your best (or worst) vacation, write a paragraph about it.*

Little People of America

full text on page 154 (cd track 25)

Introduction ❖

Little People of America can be children or adults. They can be young or old. They are people who are born with a condition called dwarfism. Dwarfism refers to people 4-foot-10 or smaller. It affects about 50,000 people in the United States. A national organization called Little People of America, Inc. is a 5000 member non-profit group that provides support for people who are short. Here is an interview with Amy Watson, age 23, who is three feet tall. She is attending a worldwide conference on dwarfism in Massachusetts.

Vocabulary ❖

1. **stature** - how tall you are; your height
2. **gene** - the basic part of a living cell that contains characteristics of one's parents
3. **conception** - the beginning or creation of life
4. **pregnancy** - the condition of a growing child in the uterus
5. **disability** - a disadvantage or handicap
6. **spinal cord** - a thick nerve that runs through the bones (spine) in the back
7. **orthopedic** - a part of medicine that specializes in problems in the bones
8. **workshops** - small groups of people who work together
9. **neurology** - the study of the nervous system and its disorders
10. **the guy scene** - where available men are

Dictation ❖

Fill in the blank with the word or words you hear. Then go over the dictation and discuss with a partner.

Reporter: I understand there are about _____ _____ at this conference.

Amy: Yes. Some of the younger little people come _____ _____ _____, who are of average stature.

Reporter: What are _____ _____ of dwarfism?

Amy: It is a chemical change within a _____ _____ that begins during conception. It is not caused by anything the parents have done during pregnancy ___ _____. Nine out of ten children born with this condition have _____- _____ _____.

Reporter: Are there _____ _____ ____ dwarfism?

Amy: Yes, but the most _____ _____ is called achondroplasia, which accounts for ____ % of all cases.

Reporter: Is dwarfism ___ _____?

Amy: We _____ _____ ____ ____ considered disabled, although some of us have spinal and orthopedic problems. Most of us have _____ _____, normal life spans, and reasonably good health.

Reporter: Coming to a conference like this is ___ _____ _____to socialize with others like yourself.

Amy: Yeah, it's wonderful because here I can find people who understand the _____- ___-_____ things I experience. At least _____ _____ ___ _____, I get to feel normal. People here instantly connect and it's like, "wow!" You could actually meet someone for a _____-_____ relationship.

Reporter: What kinds of activities _____ _____ ?

Amy: There are workshops for our _____ _____ _____who want to learn more about our condition. Medical specialists _____ _____ on topics like neurological concerns, pregnancy, and psychological _____.

Reporter: I see that there are other fun activities as well.

Amy: Uh, huh. There are_____ _____, dances, soccer games, and typical tourist trips to_____ _____.

Reporter: What's the best part for you?

Amy: The _____ _____ _____ and exchange emails with. I'm definitely going _____ _____ _____ the guy scene. Who knows, I may find someone_____, _____, and handsome!

Discussion ❖ *Talk about these issues with a partner.*

1. A person with achondroplasia has one dwarfism gene and one "average size" gene. If both parents have achondroplasia, there is a 25% chance their child will be average size. There's a 50% chance the child will be a dwarf. And there is a 25% chance the child which will die at birth or shortly afterwards. What advice do you think a doctor would give to an achondroplasic couple who want to have a family?

2. Scientists say that genetic screening for achondroplasia in fetuses is available (along with tests for other genetic defects). Do you think that this condition will become extinct in the future?

3. One term that is not acceptable in the LP (little people) community is "midget." This is an old term that used to be associated with carnival shows and circus acts. In other words, "midgets" were seen as freaks. There are other offensive words for other minority groups such as Italians, African-Americans, and Asians. Share words that you know and discuss why these words are disrespectful.

4. At the conference there are workshops touching on parental concerns such as safety issues, teasing, self-esteem, and the raising of teenagers with dwarfism. What specific types of questions do you think these parents and relatives would have for social workers and psychologists?

5. Little people often disagree over whether they are part of the disabled community. Those who say "yes, we are disabled" are working together to get the government to make new regulations with short people in mind. This is because LPs have problems at services such as ATMs and gas pumps, and would like to see their needs accommodated like those of the handicapped. What other problems do you think LPs would run into?

Writing ✤

*You are the parent of 10-year-old child in a wheelchair.
List the extra responsibilities that you would have.*

The First Americans

full text on page 155 (cd track 26)

Introduction ❖

The earliest group of people to settle in North America are sometimes called American Indians or Native Americans. They had been living in North (and South) America long before any Europeans arrived. They were, indeed, the first Americans. Here is a brief history of their conflicts with European settlers.

Vocabulary ❖

1. **archeologists** - people who study human life and civilizations
2. **scattered** - gone in all directions
3. **settle** - to move to an area and make a home
4. **harmony** - peaceful cooperation
5. **ownership** - belonging to a person or group
6. **cheat** - to do something dishonest for gain
7. **unwillingness** - refusal to accept an action
8. **reservation** - a land area set aside for native people to live on
9. **battles** - fights between enemy soldiers; struggles
10. **conflicts** - disagreements
11. **ended up** - came to
12. **mainstream** - the most popular way of thinking

Dictation ❖ *Listen and fill in the blanks. Correct and discuss with a partner.*

Archeologists believe Native Americans came from _____ 25,000 years ago. By the year ____

_____, many different groups lived ____ _____ _____ of North America. Because Indians

lived in scattered groups and _____ _____ _____ with each other, they developed

_____ _____ . They spoke _____ _____ different languages, _____

different types ____ _____ , built different _____ ____ _____ , and made

_____ _____ in different ways. Those who settled in the northern areas _____

_____ _____ . Those who settled in the _____ _____ _____ farmed. Despite

their many differences, most Indians _____ _____ _____ that people should live in

harmony _____ _____ . They believed that people should not _____ _____ because the

land, like the air, stars, and water, belonged ____ _____ . The European settlers believed in

the ownership of _____ _____ . These two very different _____ ____ _____

were the basis of the many conflicts between the Indians and the settlers.

In the early years of discovery and exploration between _____ and the mid _____ , rela-

tions with the Indians were, for the most part, _____ . But as more and more settlers ar-

rived, _____ _____ . Indian tribal leaders were _____ _____

_____ because settlers were crowding people off their land. When Indians "sold" land to the

settlers, the Indians _____ _____ _____ they were only giving whites

the right to use the land.

Many settlers _____ ____ _____ the Indian way of life and _____ _____

_____ . But others cheated them and took their land. While Indians always fought _____

_____ _____ , they were unable to stop the advance of thousands of settlers supported

by the _____ _____ . Indians won some battles, but they always _____ ____ losing

their lands.

By _____ , fighting had stopped. Finally, the government moved almost all the remaining

Indians _____ _____ . Today, however, _____ _____ _____ of the

Indians live on reservations. Those who do try to preserve their _____ _____ and

ways of life. But discrimination by non-Indians, an unwillingness by Indians to _____ _____

_____ , and a basic _____ ____ the federal government, have kept many Indians out

of the _____ of _____ life.

Discussion ❖ *Refer to the dictation in order to answer these questions with a partner.*

1. Why are there so many different Native American languages and cultures?
2. What was the basic difference in beliefs about land between the settlers and the Indians?
3. Why were Native Americans pushed farther west and eventually onto reservations?
4. Where are most Native Americans living today?
5. Many casinos are now on Indian reservation land, owned by the Indians and not regulated by the federal government. What is your opinion about this?

Writing and discussion ❖

Look up one of the following Indian tribes on the Internet. Write a summary (or five interesting facts you learned) of the article and tell the class about it.

Tribes: Hopi, Cree, Navaho, Iroquois, Mohawk, Apache, Wampanoag, Oneida, Comanche, and Arapaho. (If you want to, include one that is not listed here.)

We Shall Overcome

full text on page 156 (cd track 27)

Introduction ❖

The song "We Shall Overcome" became the song that Americans sang in their fight for racial equality. Singing helped give the civil rights protesters courage to go on. Listen to the song and sing along.

> We shall overcome
> We shall overcome
> We shall overcome some day.
> Deep in my heart
> I do believe
> We shall overcome some day.

Vocabulary ❖

1. **1950s** - Read as "nineteen fifties"
2. **segregated** - separate; a segregated school can only be used by members of one race, religion, sex, etc.
3. **discrimination** - the practice of treating a person or a group differently from another in an unfair way
4. **sit-in** - a peaceful non-violent method of protest
5. **facilities** - places or buildings used for a particular activity
6. **ideal** - a principle or standard that you want to achieve

Dictation ❖ *Write the correct word in the blank space. With a partner, correct and discuss the dictation.*

Although President Abraham Lincoln's Emancipation Proclamation set the slaves free during

_____ _____ _____ in 1865, blacks ____ _____ _____, especially in the south, still

suffered from unfair treatment because of _____ _____. Some states did not allow blacks ____

_____. Schools, buses, trains, and public businesses like theaters and restaurants were segregated

– separated into facilities for _____ _____ _____.

   Imagine being a _____ _____, _____, or child in 1950 in Mississippi. You _____

_____ _____. You could go to school with black children only. You could drink only from a separate

water fountain, use separate bathrooms, swim in a separate swimming pool, and ride at the _____

____ _____ _____.

   In the 40s and 50s, Presidents Roosevelt and Truman had said that discrimination based on race and

religion was against the ideals of _____ _____. However, it was not until 1954 that the Supreme Court said, "Separate educational facilities are inherently unequal." With this ruling,

the Civil Rights Movement _____ _____. The courts ordered schools to be desegregated.

Now blacks had government support in their fight for equality, and the Civil Rights Movement

_____ _____. It took ten years before the Civil Rights Act was passed by Congress. During that

time many black citizens were holding peaceful marches and sit-ins ____ _____ ____ get voting

rights and desegregated schools. They were often violently attacked by whites and even policemen

armed with batons, bullwhips, fire hoses, _____ _____ . But still they marched peacefully, singing

"We Shall Overcome." while the world watched ____ _____.

The song "We Shall Overcome" _____ _____ a black gospel song, became the song of

the _____ _____ movement. It was sung during the sit-ins, voter registration drives, and

protest marches of those heroic days. Since that time this song _____ _____ _____ by people

_____ _____ the world who are fighting for equality or _____ _____.

Discussion ❖ *Discuss these questions with a partner. Share your ideas with the class.*

1. Do you know of any place in the world now where facilities are still segregated?
2. Do you know of any place in the world now where every citizen doesn't have equal rights?
3. Why does this happen?
4. Are there people in your country who had to fight for their right to vote?
5. Can anyone who comes to your country as an immigrant become a citizen?
6. Do you know any song(s) that people have sung in their fight for rights or freedom?
7. Do you think that racism has disappeared in the United States?

Writing ❖ *Write a paragraph (or more) about one of the seven discussion questions.*

❄ LANGUAGE ❄

Complaining

Introduction ❄

full text on page 157 (cd track 28)

Everyone has a complaint about something. Here are a few examples of common complaints.

Vocabulary ❄

1. **gas guzzlers** - cars that "eat up" or use more gasoline than necessary
2. **strict** - expecting rules to be followed; stern
3. **suspenseful** - creating a nervous condition caused by uncertainty
4. **food poisoning** - a stomach illness caused by eating bad food
5. **weird** - strange or unusual
6. **optimist** - one who sees things positively
7. **pessimist** - one who sees things negatively

Dictation ❄
Listen and write the words you hear in the blank spaces. Then, with a partner, decide on a response to these complainers. Take the optimist's (or positive) view.

Optimists and Pessimists

Example:
(complaint) "The winters here in the Northeast are very cold."
(response)   That's true, but you can go skating and enjoy the quiet beauty of the first snowfall.

1. "The food at McDonald's _____ _____ _____.

    On the other hand, _____.

2. " _____ _____ is illogical."

    OK, but _____.

3. "There are ____ _____ _____ in the U.S."

    That's true, but _____.

4. "It's been raining for _____ _____ _____."

    Yes, but _____.

5. "American cars _____ _____ _____."

    I know, but _____.

6. "I have to pay a lot _____ _____ _____."

    Anyway, _____.

7. "My parents _____ _____ _____."

    That may be true, but_____.

Discussion and Pairwork ✤

You're walking down a busy street behind a young woman (YW) with a cell phone. You hear only her part of the conversation, of course. Can you guess what the other person (OP) is saying? Work with a partner and decide how to complete the conversation. Then share your conversations with the class.

1. Conversation One

YW: I just had lunch at that new Italian restaurant in the North End. It was terrible!

OP: _____.

YW: I tried the chicken parmesan and the chicken wasn't cooked enough. It was pink.

OP: _____.

YW: Right. I'm just glad I didn't end up in the hospital with food poisoning.

2. Conversation Two

YW: You know that teller's job I interviewed for at City Bank? Well, I didn't get it.

OP: _____.

YW: Well, the woman who interviewed me was really weird.

OP: _____.

YW: She asked me if I liked money.

OP: Really? _____.

3. Conversation Three

YW: That used car I just bought is making strange noises.

OP: _____.

YW: I did, but my mechanic couldn't find any problems.

OP: _____.

YW: Yeah, that's a good idea.

Discussion ❄

Here are some situations where people should turn off their cell phones. Work with a partner and talk about whether you have experienced these situations. Share your experiences with the class.

Part A

1. You are in a funeral home and the minister is saying a prayer for the deceased. A cell phone rings.
2. You are in the middle of an important exam. A cell phone rings.
3. You are watching a suspenseful movie in a theater. A cell phone rings.

Part B

Who's the complainer? With a partner, decide who is complaining. In some cases there is more than one possible answer.

Example: "Why don't you do the laundry this week, dear?"   Wife (to husband)

1. "This bedroom is always such a mess."   _____
2. "This car I just got is a lemon."   _____
3. "She's always wearing my clothes without permission."   _____
4. "He promised not to raise taxes and then he did."   _____
5. "The people upstairs are so noisy."   _____
6. "You really should lose 50 pounds."   _____
7. "I want everyone to be on time for class tomorrow."   _____

Idioms ❄ *Here are some common idioms or expressions that you hear when people are upset. Can you guess what they mean?*

1. Get off my back!
2. He gave me the run around.
3. I don't like being cooped up in an office all day.
4. He gets on my nerves.
5. I'm fed up with the situation.
6. Those kids drive me crazy! They're driving me out of my mind.
7. Mary got out of bed on the wrong side this morning.

Writing ❄

Today you can be an optimist or a pessimist. Write a paragraph about a good or bad experience you had and explain what you learned from this experience. Begin with an introductory sentence and then explain step by step what happened.

What's So Funny?

full text on page 157 (cd track 29)

Introduction ❋

In many cases Americans laugh at exactly the same things people in other countries laugh at. Here are two American jokes which we hope you will find funny. If you don't understand the joke, you say "I don't get it." The final line of the joke which should make you laugh is called "the punch line."

Vocabulary ❋

1. **tenant** - a person who is renting a house or apartment
2. **tuba** - a large musical instrument that you play by blowing into and that makes very loud, low sounds
3. **stomp** - to walk with heavy steps, to put your foot down very hard, especially if you're angry
4. **urgently** - very important and needing to be done immediately
5. **warning** - something that tells you that something bad, annoying, or dangerous might happen
6. **yell** - shout or say something very loudly
7. **yikes** - a meaningless word said when something frightens or shocks you

Pair Dictation ❄

In the dictation on this page and the next, work in pairs and dictate to each other. Student A will have half of the jokes and will read their part to Student B who has the other half. Student A dictates and student B writes; then student B dictates and student A writes until each joke is finished. With your partner, correct the dictation and decide which joke you think is funnier.

❄ Student A ❄

Joke 1:

"Those people upstairs _____ _____ _____," complained the tenant. "_____ _____ they stomped and banged on the floor until midnight." " _____ _____ _____ _____?" asked the landlord. "____", _____ _____ _____. "Luckily, I was playing _____ _____."

Joke 2:

As a senior citizen _____ _____ _____ _____ _____, his car phone rang. _____, he heard his wife's voice _____ _____ _____. "Herman, I just heard on the news that _____ ___ _____ _____ _____ _____ _____ on Route 280. I know you _____ _____ _____ _____, so please be careful!" " _____," _____ _____, "it's not just ONE car. _____ _____ ___ _____!"

Pair Dictation ❋

In the dictation on this page and page 89, work in pairs and dictate to each other. Student A will have half of the jokes and will read their part to Student B who has the other half. Student A dictates and student B writes; then student B dictates and student A writes until each joke is finished. With your partner, correct the dictation and decide which joke you think is funnier.

❋ Student B ❋

Joke 1:

"_____ _____ _____ are very annoying," _____ _____

_____. "Last night _____ _____ _____ _____ ___ _____ _____

_____ _____." "Did they wake you?" _____ _____ _____.

"No", replied the tenant. "_____, ___ _____ _____ my tuba."

Joke 2:

____ ___ _____ _____ was driving down the highway, _____ _____ _____

_____. Answering, ____ _____ _____ _____ _____ urgently warning him.

"_____, ___ _____ _____ ___ _____ _____ _____ there's a car going the wrong

way ____ _____ _____. ___ _____ _____ usually take Route 280, ___ _____ ___

_____!" "Yikes," yelled Herman, _____ _____ _____ _____ _____. It's hundreds of

them!"

Discussion ❋ *Discuss the following with a partner.*

1. Do you understand the two jokes?
2. Which joke do you prefer?

Writing ❋ *Find a funny joke. Turn it into a dictation. Make copies and read it to the class.*

Proverbs

full text on page 158 (cd track 30)

Introduction ❋

A proverb is a short, popular saying that expresses some common truth or thought. Every culture has them. Here are a few American ones. After you have talked about these three, share one proverb that you know with the class.

1. A picture is worth a thousand words.
2. When the cat's away, the mice will play.
3. An apple a day keeps the doctor away.

Vocabulary ❋
1. **hatch -** to come out of an egg; be born
2. **spoil -** to make bad or rotten
3. **broth -** a clear soup
4. **tricks -** actions animals are trained to do
5. **worm -** a small crawling animal with no legs
6. **hard -** difficult

Dictation ❋
Fill in the blank spaces. Correct and discuss the meaning of each proverb with a partner.

1. There's no _____ _____ _____.

2. Don't _____ _____ _____ before they're hatched.

3. First _____, first _____.

4. Love makes the world ____ _____.

5. _____ is _____.

6. _____ _____ _____ spoil the broth.

7. You can't _____ ___ _____ _____ new tricks.

8. You can't have your cake and _____ ____ _____.

9. _____ and _____.

10. The _____ _____ catches the worm.

11. The _____ _____ is the hardest.

12. The apple doesn't _____ _____ _____ from the tree.

Discussion ❋ *Share two proverbs that you know with a partner and explain what they mean.*

Cooperative Learning ❋

Work in four groups with 3, 4, or 5 students in each group. Each student finds answers to one or several proverbs and reports back to their group. Then all four groups share the answers they have found in reconfigured groups, each person responsible for all of the answers from their group.

Group One

1. Beauty is only skin deep.
2. Many hands make light work.
3. Opportunity seldom knocks twice.
4. The grass is always greener in the other person's yard.
5. The squeaky wheel gets the oil.

Group Two

1. Two heads are better than one.
2. One man's loss is another man's gain.
3. Life is just a bowl of cherries.
4. Let sleeping dogs lie.
5. It never rains but it pours.

Group Three

1. Don't put off until tomorrow what you can do today.
2. The love of money is the root of all evil.
3. All work and no play makes Jack a dull boy.
4. Don't put all your eggs in one basket.
5. To err is human, to forgive, divine.

Group Four

1. People who live in glass houses shouldn't throw stones.
2. Honesty is the best policy.
3. You don't get something for nothing.
4. A stitch in time saves nine.
5. Do unto others as you would have them do unto you.

Writing ❄

Choose a proverb that you know and write a short paragraph about it. If possible, include a personal experience in your writing.

If you prefer, write about one of these proverbs:

(from Africa): It takes a village to raise a child.

(from China): There are always ears on the other side of the wall.

Brain Teasers!

full text on page 159 (cd track 31)

Introduction ❋

Here are some tricky questions. Don't be fooled! But don't worry, you won't look foolish!

Vocabulary ❋

1. **feathers** - birds' "clothing"
2. **cement** - a material that, when mixed with water, will harden like a rock
3. **pound** - a weight of 16 ounces or 453.6 grams
4. **buried** - put in the ground after death
5. **sand piles** - little hills children make with the sand at the beach
6. **lion** - the largest wild cat
7. **tiger** - wild, striped cat
8. **attack** - to use violent force

Dictation and Discussion ❋ *After checking the dictation, try to figure out the answer with a partner.*

Example: When the Vice-President of the U.S. dies, who is the President?
Answer: The President!

1. Which is heavier, a pound of feathers, or a _____ ____ _____ ?

2. How many _____ _____ does the average person have?

3. Can a man _____ ____ _____ in northern United States be buried in Canada?

4. A little girl is playing ____ _____ _____. She is making sand piles. She has
   _____ _____ in one place and _____ _____ in another place. If she
   puts them _____ _____, how many sand piles will she have?

5. Bob ____ _____ _____ Sam. Sam is standing behind Bob at the _____
   _____. How is that possible?

6. _____ _____ _____ have a lion attack you or a tiger?

7. What word, if pronounced right, ____ _____ but if pronounced "wrong" ____
   _____ ?

8. Do you know the thing that has keys that open ____ _____, has space but ____
   _____, and allows you to enter but _____ ____ ____ ?

Riddles ❄ *(cover column B first and try to guess)*

A

1. Why do birds fly south for the winter?

2. What kind of water never freezes?

3. Who did Burger King marry?

4. Where can you always find money?

B

a. in a dictionary

b. Dairy Queen

c. it's too far to walk

d. hot water

Writing ❄ *Write five riddles and share them with the class.*

Trivia Contest

Introduction ❋   *full text on page 160 (cd track 32)*

Trivia is information that is not important but is fun to know.

Vocabulary ❋

1. **abbreviation** - shortened form of a word or phrase
2. **license plate** - a permit from the government attached to a car in the form of a piece of metal with numbers and letters on it.

Dictation ❋ *After you fill in the blank spaces, work together in pairs or small groups and answer as many questions as you can. The group with the most correct answers wins the contest.*

1. What does the abbreviation ET _____ _____ ?

2. What do people put _____, _____, and _____ dressing on?

3. What is the _____ _____ of _____ that a woman has had at one time ?

4. What do people in the United States have to do ____ _____ ____ ?

5. What is the name of the _____ _____ _____ in India ?

6. What do you do when you _____ ____ _____ ?

7. Who wrote ____ _____ _____ ?

8. What sports event takes place ____ ____ _____ ?

9. Which is the _____ _____ ?

10. What _____ do they speak in _____ ?

11. What is present in _____, _____, _____, and chocolate ?

12. What was the _____ _____ _____ and where ____ ____ _____?

13. Who does a car with the _____ ____ on the license plate _____ ____?

14. Who was both _____ and _____, but became a _____?

Cooperative Learning ❄

Work in four groups with three, four, or five students in each group. Each student finds the answers to one or several trivia questions and reports back to their group. Then all four groups share the answers they have found in newly rearranged groups, each person responsible for all of the answers from their group.

Group One

1. What is the coldest month in the US?
2. What are "Subs," "Po Boys," and "Hoagies" ?
3. What's the hardest rock?
4. Where is the smallest bone in the human body?
5. Who wrote *Julius Caesar, Macbeth,* and *Hamlet?*

Group Two

1. What is the most popular spectator sport in the world?
2. What does the modern slang word "cool" really mean?
3. End this common phrase, "See you later, ...
4. What first language is spoken by the most people in the world?
5. How can you write the words "I scream" so that they have a different meaning?

Group Three

1. How many events are there in the decathlon?
2. What are "soda" and "pop" common words for?
3. What book has been translated into the most languages?
4. What is the full term for e-mail?
5. How many words are there in the English language?

Group Four

1. What insect has been around since the time of the dinosaur?
2. What do "bucks," "fins," and "C notes" refer to?
3. What does UFO stand for?
4. What was the previous name of Thailand?
5. How much is a "baker's dozen"?

Writing ❋ *In a group, write a mini trivia contest (5 questions) for your classmates.*

1.

2.

3.

4.

5.

What's in a Name?

full text on page 161 (cd track 33)

Introduction ❄

Parents spend a lot of time deciding on a name for a baby yet to be born. Go into any bookstore and there are many books of names and their meanings for prospective parents to look through.

Vocabulary ❄

1. **prospective** - likely to be
2. **ethnic** - relating to a particular race, tribe, or nation
3. **incredibly** - unbelievably

Dictation ❄ *Write the correct word or number in the blank space. With a partner, correct and discuss the dictation.*

"What's in a name?" wrote Shakespeare. "A rose by any other name would smell as sweet."

_____, we give great importance to names. In some _____ the baby

____ _____ the name of a favorite _____ who has died. In other _____, the

first- born _____ child receives the same name as his father with one _____ _____. In

an English-speaking culture, if the father is Wilson Smith, Sr. (Senior), the baby becomes Wilson Smith, Jr.

(Junior).   When Wilson Smith, Jr., has a baby, that baby may be called Wilson Smith, III (the third).

Some people name their children after _____ _____ or famous people. In the 1940s

many girls named Shirley _____ _____ after a child actress, Shirley Temple. Nowadays we

_____ _____ children named Celine and Brad.

When people from other _____ come to the United States, _____ as international

students or as _____, they often change their names and _____ English names.

They do this _____ _____ reasons. First, English speakers may have _____

understanding and _____ their names correctly. Second, people may have _____

_____ _____ their names. Third, because they are in a new country, they may want

to change their _____ and begin with a new name.

In a recent discussion among ESL teachers, one teacher said, "For Koreans, names are incredibly

_____, not to be thrown _____ lightly, and we are not doing right by our Korean

students if we _____ them to _____ English names. It is a form of _____

to learn the Korean names correctly." Another teacher responded, "I have a problem with Korean and

Chinese names. They all seem to be three syllables. They are not _____ identifiable to me as

_____ or _____. Korean names are so similar that I cannot _____ _____ apart in my

mind for at least the first four or five weeks of class, no matter _____ _____ ___ _____. I know

who the students are. I just _____ ____ their names."

Discussion ❄ *Discuss these questions with a partner. Share your ideas with the class.*

1. Do you know the meaning of your name? What is it?
2. Have your parents ever told you why they gave you your particular name?
3. Have you ever taken a new name? Why and how did you choose it?
4. Are you upset when an English speaker does not pronounce your name correctly? Do you correct them?

Writing ❄ *Choose **one** of the above topics or one of the two that follow to write about.*

1. When babies are given names, there is often a religious or cultural ceremony performed at the same time. If this is done in your country, discuss and describe it.

2. When people marry in the US there may be a change of names. For example, when Barbara McDonald marries Richard Cogan she can become Barbara Cogan or she can become Barbara Cogan-McDonald or Barbara McDonald-Cogan (Richard can become Richard McDonald-Cogan or Richard Cogan-McDonald). She can also remain Barbara McDonald. Describe how names change in your family when people get married.

❖ FOOD, HEALTH, AND THE ENVIRONMENT ❖

Home Remedies

full text on page 162 (cd track 34)

Introduction ❖

We like simple solutions to problems of serious illness when we're not feeling well. For example our grandmothers told us to feed a cold and starve a fever, and to tie garlic around our neck to help prevent that cold. Some of these suggestions seem silly to us today, but many of them have proved to have some scientific basis. In 2003 when the SARS epidemic first appeared, some Koreans had a simple answer for how to prevent it. Find out about it in the dictation.

Vocabulary ❖

1. **epidemic** - a large number of cases of a disease happening at the same time
2. **starve** - to die because you do not have enough to eat
3. **cabbage** - a large round vegetable with thick green or purple leaves
4. **garlic** - a plant like a small onion with a very strong taste used in cooking
5. **chili pepper** - a small type of pepper with a very strong spicy taste
6. **fermented** - a chemical change as when sugar is converted into alcohol
7. **stocking up** - accumulating goods to keep in reserve
8. **curative powers** - ability to cure illness
9. **theory** - a set of ideas created to explain something
10. **over-the-counter** - medicines, like aspirin, that you can buy without a prescription

Dictation ❖ *Fill in the blanks with the words you hear. Correct and discuss the dictation with a partner.*

It is just fermented cabbage, garlic, and chili peppers, _____ _____ are buying _____

_____ of kimchi, hoping Korea's _____ _____ is really a wonder drug. Southeast

Asians are _____ ____ on it. It's very _____ in China. And South Koreans, _____

_____ ____ with every meal, are buying more than usual, hoping that word of its curative powers

will make it famous.

"___ _____ _____ a meal without kimchi," said a housewife. "_____ _____

my children _____ a lot more of it these days. I certainly believe that they did not get SARS because

they eat ___ _____ ____ _____."

A Korean scientist says this theory may be difficult to prove, but that doesn't mean ____ _____

_____.

Discussion ✤ *With a partner, discuss the following questions.*

1. Folk medicine beliefs and practices differ from culture to culture. They are passed on from person to person by word of mouth and imitation. Most cures and remedies depend on what is close at hand to treat illnesses. They include things like soda, garlic, sugar, whiskey, vinegar, plants, mud, vodka, and mustard.   Here are some examples:
   - for hair loss, rub your head with half an onion before you go any balder.
   - for a sore throat, mash an onion into pulp and add a little water until you have onion juice and gargle. (Needless to say, don't do this before a date.)

2. What remedies have you heard about from your parents or grandparents that are traditional, rather than something your doctor prescribes or that you buy over the counter at a pharmacy?

3. Have you ever tried one of these remedies?

Idioms ✤

Here are some common idioms or expressions. Can you and your partner guess what they mean?

1. Give someone a taste of their own medicine.
2. Laughter is the best medicine.
3. She's a real pill.
4. That's a bitter pill to swallow.

Writing ✤ *Choose **one** of the following topics.*

1. Why do people use folk remedies? One reason may be that they can't afford a doctor. What are some other reasons? List as many reasons as you can.
2. Make a list of folk medicine recipes that you and your classmates know about.

Chocoholics, Unite!

full text on page 162 (cd track 35)

Introduction ❖

"Hi, my name is Eleanor and I am addicted to chocolate. I think about chocolate always, except when I'm asleep and then I dream about chocolate!"

"In the beginning there was a word, and the word was chocolate, and it was good."

Vocabulary ❖

1. **crave -** to desire greatly; to need right away
2. **mood -** an emotional state
3. **addict -** a person physically or emotionally dependent on a substance
4. **currency -** the money used to pay for goods and services
5. **sinful -** against religious ideas of what is right

Dictation ❖

After you have filled in the words, work with a partner and decide if the statements are fact or opinion. Write F for fact and O for opinion.

___ 1. Chocolate from Belgium ____ _____ _____.

___ 2. People crave chocolate more than _____ _____ _____.

___ 3. Chocolate _____ ____ _____ associated with mood, emotion, and addiction.

___ 4. Chocolate is sinful because it has lots of _____ _____ _____.

___ 5. Chocolate lovers _____ _____ _____ for almost 3000 years.

___ 6. Chocolate comes from cacao beans, and ____ _____ _____ was used as a form of currency.

___ 7. _____ _____ _____ cacao trees in Africa, Southeast Asia, and South and Central America.

___ 8. You can _____ _____ _____ when you are depressed or stressed.

Discussion ❖

Part A. *With a partner, talk about these addictions. Do you have one or know someone who does? Explain! Can you add some to the list?*

1. shopaholic
2. netaholic
3. chocoholic
4. TV addict
5. soda addict
6. smoker
7. alcoholic
8. drug addict
9. workaholic

Part B. *Talk about the meanings of these "addiction" idioms and expressions with the class.*

1. Cigarettes run his life.
2. She can't kick the habit.
3. I'm hooked on the Internet.
4. She needs a fix.
5. He's having a nicotine fit.
6. You got a buzz from the drink.
7. I shop till I drop.

Writing ❖

Pretend there is someone you know who is hooked on shopping. Write a letter to them and give suggestions that will help this person kick the habit. Before you write, talk about the letter with a partner.

Dear _____,
      (friend's name)

Your friend,

_____
(your name)

Eat That Insect?

full text on page 163 (cd track 36)

Introduction ❖

David Gordon, a science writer and author of *Eat-A-Bug Cookbook,* says that many insects are not only good-tasting but also good for you. He tasted his first bug ten years ago at a Seattle Museum event where Chex party mix was served with oven-baked crickets. To learn more about entomophagy, or bug-eating, try the dictation!

Vocabulary ❖

caterpillar

butterfly

ladybug

termite

wasp

cricket

ant

grasshopper

mealworm

Pair Dictation ❖

In the dictation here and on the next page, work in pairs and dictate to each other. Student A will have half of the article and will read their lines to student B, who has the other half. Student A dictates and Student B writes, then Student B dictates and A writes until the passage is complete. Do not look at each other's pages!

❖ Student A ❖

Ladybugs are cute _____ _____ _____ _____, but most people who

come face to face _____ ____ _____ have one thought: _____ ___ ___! David

Gordon takes a different approach. ___ _____ _____ _____ _____ _____.

He thinks insects are a valuable, _____, _____ _____ _____

of nutrition. "If you're eating hot dogs, _____ _____ _____ _____ way

weirder than a grasshopper," said Gordon ____ ___ _____ _____ _____

_____ in an elementary school cafeteria. ___ _____ _____ ___ _____

grasshopper kebabs, fried crickets, and grilled mealworms. _____ _____ _____

_____ _____ _____ from eating bugs, _____ _____ _____

_____ _____ _____ _____ _____ _____! But beware! Not all bugs taste

good, ____ _____ _____ _____, especially caterpillars. _____ _____

_____ _____ _____ do not want to eat them, which is why _____ _____

_____ _____ _____ _____ _____ thousands of trees each year.

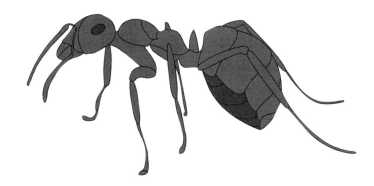

Pair Dictation ❖

In the dictation here and on page 107, work in pairs and dictate to each other. Student A will have half of the article and will read their lines to student B, who has the other half. Student A dictates and Student B writes, then Student B dictates and A writes until the passage is complete. Do not look at each other's pages!

❖ Student B ❖

_____ _____ _____ and butterflies are pretty, _____ _____ _____ _____

_____ _____ ___ _____ with an insect _____ ____ _____: Step on it!

_____ _____ _____ __ _____ _____. He cooks bugs and

eats them. ____ _____ _____ _____ ____ _____, underused,

and delicious source ___ _____. " ___ _____ _____ ____ _____,

you're eating stuff that's _____ _____ _____ __ _____," _____

_____ as he demonstrated his cooking skills ___ ___ _____ _____

_____. On his grill he prepared _____ _____, _____

_____, _____ _____ _____. School rules prevented the children

_____ _____ _____, but teachers tried them and thought they were tasty! _____

_____! _____ _____ _____ _____ _____, and some are poisonous, _____

_____ _____. Even birds and other animals ___ _____ _____ ___

_____ _____, _____ ___ _____ some caterpillars can eat and destroy _____

___ _____ _____ _____.

Discussion ❖ *Work with a partner and talk about these questions. Share your ideas with the class.*

1. How do you think the children in the school reacted when Gordon offered the cooked insects to the teachers?

2. Eating bugs is uncommon in the U.S., Europe, and Canada but routine in many other countries. For example, in Mexico people eat grasshoppers; in Indonesia people eat giant water bugs; in Africa they eat termites; in Japan they eat canned wasps; and in South Korea, they eat canned silkworm pupae. Have you tried any strange foods, such as frogs' legs, turtle soup, smoked dog, or chocolate ants?

3. Pretend that your boss invites you to dinner and serves grasshopper kebab. How would you react?

4. Is there one food that you just can't eat?

Insect Idioms and Expressions ❖ *Talk about the meanings of these sentences.*

1. He bugs me.
2. I told her to bug off.
3. I put a bug in his ear.
4. The phone was bugged.
5. He wormed his way into the conversation.
6. She has a bee in her bonnet.

Do you know that . . .

1. There are more kinds of beetles on earth than any other living creature.
2. Butterflies taste with their hind feet.
3. A cockroach can live several weeks with its head cut off.
4. An ant can lift 50 times its own weight.
5. Ants, ounce for ounce, contain twice as much protein as a sirloin steak.

Writing ❖ *Choose **one** of the following.*

1. Cockroaches have long been used in medicinal teas and treatments. Do some research on these insects and write a summary of interesting facts you learned.

2. Find out what ingredients there are in a hot dog. Are they "weird" as Gordon suggests? Explain.

3. Find five interesting facts about insects (not listed above) and bring them to class to share.

What Do You Eat?

full text on page 164 (cd track 37)

Introduction ❖

A recent poll gives us a look at when we eat, where we eat, what we eat, and how often we eat. Do you eat breakfast? Where do you eat it, and what do you eat?

Vocabulary ❖

1. **two thirds** - 2/3 (66.666%)
2. **three-fourths** - 3/4 (75%)
3. **two out of three** - another way of saying two thirds
4. **snack** - food that is eaten between meals
5. **slice** - a thin piece cut from a larger piece, for example, a slice of bread
6. **nibble** - to eat a little or with small quick bites
7. **prime time** - the time of night when more people watch television

Dictation ❖ *Listen and write the words you hear in the blank spaces. Correct and discuss with a partner.*

Breakfast. During the work week, _____-_____ of Americans eat breakfast, _____-_____ of them at home. About _____ ____ _____ eats breakfast at work: _____ ____ _____while driving or commuting. The most popular breakfast is _____ or _____ cereal (67%), followed by _____, or muffins, or bagels (____ ____), and eggs (____ ____). _____-_____ also snack on cereal, and _____ _____ admit they eat cereal for dinner ... sometimes.

Weekends. On _____ and Sunday, _____ _____ of us eat breakfast at home. Eggs are the _____ Sunday breakfast for more than _____. Bacon, ham, or sausages are nearly as _____; so are pancakes or waffles.

Lunch. Sandwiches _____ _____ at midday. _____ in _____ of us put our food between two _____ of bread. _____ ____ _____ eats _____ _____.

Dinner. About _____ ____ _____ who bring home _____ food said they prefer everything ready-to-eat, rather than also having a side dish prepared at home. _____ is the favorite food-to-go (the choice of _____ _____), followed by _____food (_____) and _____ _____ such as hamburgers or tacos (_____ _____).

Snacks. Evening is _____ _____ for snackers. Nearly _____-_____ of Americans snack after dinner (_____ in front of the ____), and _____ _____ nibble all day long.

Discussion ❖ *Discuss these questions with a partner. Then share your ideas with the class.*

1. Based on this dictation and your own experience, do you think Americans eat well?
2. Has your way of eating changed recently? How?
3. What are some of the foods that are new to you that you like?
4. What are some of the foods you grew up with that Americans don't know about?

Discussion ❖ *Discuss these questions with a partner. Then share your ideas with the class.*

It's 9:00 p.m. You decide that you're hungry and you want a snack. Below are some foods that you can choose from. Which of the following do you think are the three healthiest snacks to have? Which three are the unhealthiest? Which do you think you personally would choose and why?

a small box of raisins	a package of three Oreo cookies
a large apple	a bowl of Cheerios and milk
a small bag of potato chips	a bowl of frosted flakes and milk
a small bag of M&Ms	a donut
a cup of hot cocoa	crackers and cheese
a big bowl of popcorn	a small bag of unsalted nuts
a peanut butter and jelly sandwich	a dish of ice cream

Writing ❖ *Describe your favorite meal. Write about when you eat it, how it tastes, how it is prepared, and why it is your favorite.*

Save Our Planet Award

full text on page 165 (cd track 38)

Introduction ❖

Do you think it is important to do something about pollution? Of course you do! We want our children to grow up in a healthy environment. Read and check (✔) the items you or your family can do to help save our planet. Talk about these items with the class.

(   ) take the bus or subway to save gasoline and lower air pollution
(   ) carpool to work or school to reduce traffic
(   ) take shorter showers to save water
(   ) turn down or turn off the air conditioner when you are not in the room to save electricity
(   ) recycle newspapers, bottles, and cans to save paper, glass, and metal
(   ) use low-energy light bulbs to save electricity
(   ) buy an electric-powered (or semi-electric) car to save on gasoline

Vocabulary ❖

1. **recycling** - saving things and using them again
2. **volunteer** - to offer to do something without pay
3. **reservoir** - a pond or lake that is used for drinking water
4. **leak** - to pass through an opening or hole that should not be there
5. **pollution** - putting dangerous substances or products into the air or water
6. **carpool** - a group of people who share a car and expenses to get to work
7. **pesticide** - a chemical preparation for destroying plant or animal pests
8. **plastic** - a strong, lightweight material made in a chemical process from oil or coal
9. **trash** - garbage; waste material
10. **dump** - a place where you put trash (dumping - dropping carelessly)
11. **hazardous waste** - dangerous materials
12. **decompose** - to rot; decay

Dictation and Discussion ❖

There are millions of people who want to save the environment! Some of them spend a lot of extra time volunteering to clean up the ocean, beaches, land, and roads. Every year, the Mayor of Greenland City, Mary Travis, gives a "Save the Planet" award to a group of people or an individual who helped keep their beautiful city clean and safe. You and your classmates will recommend a winner to Mayor Travis. Here are the five finalists.

Note: The city, the award, and the finalists are fictitious.

On the next page, fill in the blank spaces with the word or words you hear. Then discuss each candidate for the award with a partner. After you have chosen your winner, share your decision with the class. Then discuss all the decisions and vote for one winner.

1. The Teen Team. This _____ ____ _____ from Greenland Middle School saw a TV show about how plastic trash on beaches and ____ _____ _____ kills a million sea birds and fish every year. They organized a group of 15 student volunteers to _____ _____, plastic bags, and plastic containers from their city's beaches every month. This has _____ _____ _____ of many birds and fish.

2. Erin Brockton. Erin and her children discovered that ___ _____ _____ in Greenland had been dumping poisonous chemicals in an _____ _____ near her neighborhood. Some of the poison had leaked into the reservoir where the town gets its _____ _____. Many people got sick. After months ____ _____, Erin forced the paper company to find other, safer ways ____ _____ _____ ____ the waste.

3. VFR (Volunteers for Recycling). These people spend a lot of time at _____ _____ _____. Why? Because they want to help Greenland residents _____ _____ _____, bottles, and cans. They also organized a "swap shop" at the dump where people could leave _____ _____ _____ _____, TVs, computers, and other _____ _____. Then, people who need them can get them free. Their work has saved the town _____ ____ _____.

4. Ray Burrows and Arthur Clark are biologists _____ _____ ____ the Greenland Labs. Burrows and Clark believe that pesticides _____ _____ _____. They want farmers to stop using chemical pesticides on their _____ _____ _____. They are getting farmers ____ _____ _____ insects that eat the insects that eat farmers' vegetables and fruits.

5. The Green Group. A group of adults and teens learned that many people in the city were dumping _____ _____down the drain in their homes and into the sewer system. This is serious because it pollutes the city's_____. Many people can get sick from drinking water _____ ____ _____ from the dumping of motor oil, oven cleaners, _____ _____, and other dangerous chemicals. The Green Group organized two "hazardous waste" days a year at _____ _____ _____, where citizens can leave their products.

Discussion ❖ *With a partner, discuss these items. Share your ideas with the class.*

1. You want your friend to consider buying a hybrid car. This is a car that runs on electricity and gasoline. Your friend is not crazy about the idea because the car is a little more expensive than the other cars. What arguments can you use to help convince them?

2. Your sister has a new baby and is using disposable diapers. These diapers use up 1,265,000 metric tons of wood pulp and 65,000 metric tons of plastic that can take up to 500 years to decompose in a city dump. Can you convince your sister to use cloth diapers?

3. The orangutan, a large ape, is now an endangered species. There are many other animals in the world that are endangered. Can you name any? What can governments do to stop animal extinction?

Read ❖ *You can make a difference!*

- If we recycle our Sunday papers, we can save over 500,000 trees every week.

- If every commuter car carried just one more passenger, we would save 600,000 gallons of gasoline and keep 12 million pounds of "greenhouse gases" out of the air every day.

- If we all installed "low-flow" shower heads, we could save billions of gallons of water every year.

Discussion ❖ *With a partner talk about the following:*

1. Do you have any environmental problems in your country or the city you are living in now?

2. What are people doing in your city about environmental problems?

3. Do you know of any endangered animals?

4. How do you feel when you see or hear about environmental problems?

Writing ✤ *Write about A or B, below.*

A. Choose **one** of the questions in the preceding discussion and write a paragraph about it.

B. Write a paragraph explaining whom you chose as the finalist for the Save the Planet Award and why.

✳ Sports ✳

Venus and Serena Williams, Tennis Stars

full text on page 166 (cd track 39)

Introduction ✳

It has been several years since Venus and Serena Williams, two African-American sisters, became famous. Their style, as well as their athletic talent, have made them two of the world's most visible women. This is surprising, since the sisters' hometown of Compton, California, eight miles south of Los Angeles, is often associated with drugs, gangs, and violence, not tennis, which is usually considered a wealthy white person's sport.

In the fall of 2000 both sisters represented the United States at the Olympic games in Sydney, Australia. In 2001 the sisters played against each other in the United States Open and again in the finals of the French Open. This was extraordinary because both sisters were so talented, and because they were African-American.

Vocabulary ✳

1. **visible** - seen by others
2. **wealthy** - rich
3. **United States Open** - famous yearly tennis competition
4. **rivals** - people who compete with each other in order to win

Dictogloss ✳ *Listen to a complete sentence only once and write down the words you can remember. With a partner try to reconstruct the sentence in writing as accurately as possible.*

1.

2.

3.

4.

5.

Discussion ✳ *Discuss these questions with a partner. Share your ideas with the class.*

1. Do you play a competitive sport or did you play one in the past?

2. Do you think you're a competitive person? Why?

3. Do you think it's good for parents to insist that their children practice a sport or practice a musical instrument for many hours every day? Do you wish that your parents had made you do this?

Writing ✳

With hours of practice every day from the time one is very young, anyone can become a top athlete or a great musician. Write about whether you agree or disagree with this statement, and why.

Alex Rodriguez, Baseball Player

full text on page 167 (cd track 40)

Introduction ✳

Alex Rodriguez, or A-Rod as he is known in the sports community, is one of the best baseball players in today's major leagues. He is also one of the highest-paid players with a salary of $22,000,000 a year! He played for the Seattle Mariners and the Texas Rangers and is now with the New York Yankees.

Vocabulary ✳

1. **fielder** - a player who is defending against a batter
2. **major league** - a professional group of baseball players; there are two: American and National
3. **acrobatic** - jumping, running, and flying through the air
4. **home run** - hitting the ball outside the field of play, allowing the batter time to run around all the bases and back "home" to score a run.

Dictogloss ✳

Listen to a complete sentence only once and write down the words you can remember on a separate piece of paper. With a partner, try to reconstruct the entire sentence and write it below.

1.

2.

3.

4.

5.

6.

Discussion ✳ *With a partner, discuss these questions.*

1. Do you think superstar baseball players like A-Rod should make so much money? Why or why not?

   Consider: (A) Sports players seldom play after age 40. What kind of work can they find at this time in their lives, since they are not ready for the rocking chair?

   (B) The New York Yankees are the richest team in the U.S. and can afford to pay the highest salaries.

2. Do you think there should be a limit to the high salaries? What is the danger of not having a limit?

3. Baseball players on American teams come from many countries. Can you name a few? (A-Rod's parents were born in the Dominican Republic.)

   Example: The Dominican Republic – Pedro Martinez and David Ortiz.

Writing ✳ *Write about a famous sports figure that you admire.*

Lacrosse

full text on page 167 (cd track 41)

Introduction ✳

The sport of lacrosse looks like a combination of basketball, soccer, and hockey. It is considered to be North America's first sport -- a game developed by many Native American nations, it was particularly popular among the First Nations of Canada. It is now one of the fastest-growing team sports in the United States.

With a partner, put this brief history of lacrosse in order from the earliest facts to the latest. The first one is done for you.

(   ) Men's and women's lacrosse were played under the same rules until the mid-1930s.

(1) Lacrosse was first played centuries ago by North American Indians in preparation for war.

(   ) Women's lacrosse in the U.S. was formed in 1926 at a school in Maryland.

(   ) Lacrosse games evolved in Ontario, Canada, and in the U.S. in the 1600s.

(   ) Those earliest games had as many as 1,000 players per side, from the same or different tribes.

(   ) Lacrosse is currently a national sport with more than 250,000 active players.

(   ) French-Canadian dentist George Beers standardized the game in 1867 with a new set of rules.

Vocabulary ✳

1. **scoop** - pick up the ball with the lacrosse stick's net.
2. **agile** - quick and skillful in movement
3. **financial reward** - money earned for doing something
4. **violent** - dangerous

Dictation ✳

After you have filled in the blanks, work with a partner and decide if the statements are fact or opinion.
Write F for fact or O for opinion on the line. Discuss your answers.

____ 1. Lacrosse is played _____ ____ _____, the crosse, and the players need to

know how to _____, _____, and scoop.

____ 2. Lacrosse is a fast-paced sport and _____ ____ _____.

____ 3. _____ _____ _____ _____ than men because they are more agile.

____ 4. Most lacrosse players play for _____ ____ _____ _____ rather than for financial reward.

____ 5. Women's lacrosse is the best sport ____ _____ _____.

____ 6. Lacrosse is ___ _____ _____.

____ 7. Professional lacrosse in the U.S. has different rules and ____ _____ _____.

Discussion ✳ *With a partner, discuss these questions. Share your answers with the class.*

1. What sports do people play in other countries?
   What is the most popular sport in those countries?

2. Women are participating much more in school sports in North America.
   Is this happening elsewhere?

3. Who are some famous athletes from your country? Do they make a lot of money?

Cooperative Learning ✳

Work in four groups of three, four, or five students. Using an encyclopedia or the Internet, each student finds out about one or more sports listed below and reports back to their group. Then all four groups present what they have learned.

Group 1	*Group 2*	*Group 3*	*Group 4*
1. croquet	1. rugby	1. rounders	1. petanque
2. paragliding	2. curling	2. futsal	2. hoop takraw
3. goalball	3. skydiving	3. disc golf	3. ultimate frisbee
4. haggi hurling	4. kabbadi	4. muay Thai	4. wiffleball
5. skeet shooting	5. endurance riding	5. hang gliding	5. fencing

Writing ✳

Option 1:

Choose one of these famous Americans with some Native American Indian ancestry. Write a paragraph about them.

1. Jesse Jackson	4. Rita Coolidge
2. Johnny Depp	5. Angelina Jolie
3. Buffy Sainte Marie	6. Jimi Hendrix

Option 2:

Choose another sport that you know about and write a fact/opinion dictation similar to the one on the previous page.

Violent Sports or Violent Fans?

full text on page 168 (cd track 42)

Introduction ✳

Have you ever gone to a football or hockey game and seen violent behavior by people who are watching the game? Have you ever heard fans shouting bad language at players, coaches, and other officials? Have you ever seen victory celebrations turn ugly? Here are two actual crimes that took place during and after a sports event.

Vocabulary ✳

1. **argument** - disagreement
2. **witness** - to see an incident
3. **punishment** - a penalty for doing something wrong
4. **aggressive** - unfriendly; hostile
5. **manslaughter** - accidental killing
6. **ban** - prohibit

Dictation ✳ *Fill in the spaces with the word or words you hear. Then, with a partner, decide what kind of punishment these people should get for their actions.*

Case 1. A "hockey dad" _____ _____ an argument with the coach of his_____ _____. The argument led to ___ _____ _____ after the game. The hockey dad was so angry that he brutally attacked the coach. The coach died _____ _____ _____ from the injuries he suffered. There were many witnesses to the fight. The hockey dad_____ ____ _____. What kind of punishment do you think ____ _____ _____?

Case 2. When a football team won the Super Bowl, there was ____ _____ _____ in their home city. _____ of happy people were in the streets. Many had been drinking, however, and the crowd got _____ ___ _____. People started overturning cars parked along the streets. One car owner, a university student, was afraid that his car would be destroyed ____ _____ _____, so he got in his car and tried to _____ _____. In his nervous condition he didn't see a student _____ _____ _____. He hit the student and the student died. _____ _____ _____ went to court. This is a case of manslaughter. _____ _____ ____ punishment do you think he should receive?

Discussion and Writing ✳

*Talk about these issues with a partner. Then choose **one** topic to write about.*

1. Do you think that football, boxing, and hockey will ever be banned as sports? Why or why not?

2. Do you think that children become more aggressive after watching violent programs on TV?

3. Give some examples of non-contact/non-combative sports that provide entertainment for thousands of people all over the world.

Movie: Bend It Like Beckham

full text on page 169 (cd track 43)

Introduction ✳

David Beckham is a famous soccer player. Fans love him and young soccer players idolize him. In the movie, *Bend It Like Beckham,* two high-school-aged girls dream of someday playing just like Beckham. They want to play their best and perhaps make soccer a full-time career, even though their parents may not approve. Soccer players often have to bend their knees to score goals. The "bend" in this movie refers to making the ball bend into the net around the other players. Beckham is noted for being able to bend the ball around a line of opposing players.

Vocabulary ✳

1. **fan** - an admirer; someone who loves and respects a famous person or team
2. **idolize** - to admire greatly; to worship; to look up to
3. **talent** - the ability to do something well
4. **footsteps** - the sound of feet hitting a surface
5. **coach** - a person who leads, teaches, and trains people in sports
6. **protective** - concerned about the safety of; sheltering
7. **restricted** - limited in use or availability
8. **compete** - to participate in a game
9. **team** - two or more people playing the same sport together
10. **on her own terms** - independently

Dictation ✳ *Summary of the movie. Fill in the blanks with the words you hear. Correct and discuss the dictation with a partner.*

Bend It Like Beckham is _____ _____ ___ a young Indian immigrant, Jess Bhamra, who lives in London with her protective and _____ _____. She plays soccer for fun in a park with her friends, and Beckham ___ ____ _____. She is a talented _____ _____ in her own right, but her parents have other plans for their_____ _____. They expect Jess to follow in the footsteps of her sister, Pinky, who is _____ ___ _____ in a traditional Indian wedding.

Early in the film, Jess meets Jules, a girl her age who plays for a local _____ _____ _____. Jules thinks Jess would be a good teammate and asks Jess to join up. Jess agrees and _____ _____ _____ that she is a star player. But she doesn't _____ _____ _____ because she knows they would not approve. As a team member, she _____ ____ _____ and competes in out-of-town games that _____ _____ _____ ___ her small, restricted world. To add romantic interest, both Jess and Jules _____ ___ _____with their young soccer coach. As the movie progresses, Jess has to _____ _____ _____ if she should follow her parents' wishes or live her life on _____ _____ _____. It is a delightful coming-of-age film which also allows us to look at _____ _____ ___ _____.

Role Plays ✳

Work in groups of three or four. Each group will create one of the scenes below and act it out for the class. You have 15 minutes to create and practice. No writing is necessary. Decide what role you are going to play and what you are going to say as the scene develops. Each person should assume a role and a point of view.

To prepare for the scene, decide:
   a. what the facts are, where the scene is taking place, and who the people are in the scene.
   b. what the problem is and what might happen if this problem is not settled.

Scene 1: A girl wants to go to college to study music. Her parents want her to study business so that she can work in their jewelry store with them.

Scene 2: A teenager wants to see the movie "Sex and the Single Girl." Her parents do not think this is a good idea.

Scene 3: A mother overhears her teenage daughter on the phone talking about going to the mall to meet "boys" on a Thursday night.

Scene 4: Julio, who came to the U.S. years ago, is in love and wants to marry an American. His parents want him to marry someone from his own country and religion.

Discussion ✳ *With a partner, talk about a time when you disagreed with a family member. What was the problem? How did you resolve it?*

Writing ✳

Write a paragraph about your disagreement with a family member. Remember to write an introductory sentence, such as

I once had a big argument with my . . .

Index to Dictation Types

The Full Texts of the Articles Used as Interactive Dictations

The Full Texts of the Dictations

Made. . . Where?
(Pair Dictation)   *dictation page 1 (cd track 1)*

Introduction ❀   (*Information for teachers*)

1. About one-third of Americans own foreign cars. In some areas of the U.S. the percentage can vary. For example, in Detroit, Michigan, the center of the American car industry, a smaller percentage of foreign cars can be found. Parts of foreign cars are manufactured in the U.S.

2. Toyota is the leading foreign car company in sales in the U.S.

Pair Dictation - Students A and B ❀

Bill Smith started the day early. He set his alarm clock (made in Japan) for six o'clock, a.m. While his coffeepot (made in China) was perking, he shaved with his electric razor (made in Hong Kong). He put on a dress shirt (made in Sri Lanka), designer jeans (made in Singapore), and tennis shoes (made in Korea).

After he cooked his breakfast in his new electric fryer (made in India), he sat down with his calculator (made in Mexico) to see how much he could spend today.

After he set his watch (made in Taiwan) to the radio (made in India), he got in his car (made in Germany) and continued his search for a good-paying American job. At the end of yet another discouraging and fruitless day, Bill decided to relax for a while. He put on his sandals (made in Brazil), poured himself a glass of wine (made in France), and turned on the TV (made in Indonesia), and then wondered why he couldn't find a good-paying job in America!

Taxes and Take-Home Pay
(Partial Dictation)
dictation page 5 (cd track 2)

T   1. An average American working couple pays **38**% of their **total income** in taxes every year.

Not all of the 38% is paid as income tax, however. About 15% of that is income taxes, but Americans also have to pay sales tax, excise tax, property tax, social security tax, and rooms and meals taxes as well.

T   2. If you make **less than $4000** a year, you do not have to pay taxes.

F   3. The United States is the country with **the highest taxes.**

      Sweden: 53%, France: 40%

T   4. **Where you live** can affect the amount of tax you pay. Not all states have a state income tax and the percent of the state tax differs: for example, PA - 2.8%, MA- 5.3%, eight others have no state income tax.

F   5. Married and middle-aged people pay more in income tax than the **single and young.**

The single and young often have lifestyles that expose them to the full force of taxes. They usually rent instead of buying homes so they can't take deductions for property taxes and interest on mortgage payments.

T   6. People with a salary between **$15,000** and **$50,000** pay more to the government than people who make more than $50,000.

The upper income group, though richer, pays only about 1/4 of total income taxes.

F   7. People who make the same income pay **the same amount** of income tax.

Deductions for medical bills, dependents, etc. make the difference. A man who has a wife and six children and has a mortgage on his house and earns $45,000 pays less in taxes than a man who is not married, rents an apartment, and makes the same salary.

States with no state income tax: Alaska, Florida, Nevada, South Dakota, Texas, Wyoming, New Hampshire, Tennessee

Do You Want to Be a Nurse?
(Prediction Dictation)

dictation page 7 (cd track 3)

I think it's great that you **are** considering nursing as a career, but I would look **very** closely at the impact it can have on your personal **life**. I don't **want** to be negative, **but** a lot of people look at **nursing** as a well-paying **job** without finding out what the job really **is**. Nursing is a 24/7 commitment. We are expected to **work** weekends and **holidays**, and there is a mandatory overtime in some facilities. This means if **the** second shift calls in sick, **you** have to stay to cover the floor. You may **not** always get the vacation you request. You **have** two children; are you prepared **to work** Christmas and **Thanksgiving?** You will be expected **to**. **I've** been a nurse for 25 **years,** and I couldn't see myself doing **anything else**. However, nursing is not for **everyone**. You **have to** deal with very ill people, bodily fluids, unreasonable families **and** doctors, and it can be very stressful at times. However, on the plus side, you do **make** a difference in people's lives, and it's **great** to see them get well. Also it's possible to **change** the area of your work. You **can** do home care, intensive care, rehabilitation, pediatrics, maternity, or -- that is the great thing **about** nursing -- you aren't stuck doing the same **thing.** There are always other options.

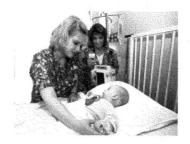

Buying a Used Car
(Note Taking) *dictation page 12 (cd track 4)*

(Because this is the first note-taking type of dictation your students will encounter, you may want to do the first one together with the class.)

Paulina, age 27, came from Brazil two years ago and has been driving for eight years, both in Brazil and in the U.S. She makes $3000 a month, but her take-home pay is $2000 a month. Her monthly living expenses, including rent, food, and utilities, are $1800. She is looking at a used car in the $8000 price range. She has the required 20% or $1600 for a down payment to the bank. She is going to pay the balance of $6400 with a three-year loan at 8% interest. Her credit record in the U.S. is good. She would have to pay the bank $200 a month (interest and principal). Her car insurance is $100 a month.

Sammy, age 22, arrived from Lebanon six months ago and he has been driving for six years. His present salary as a mechanic is $2333 a month and his take-home pay is $1500 a month. He lives with his family, so he doesn't have any monthly expenses. His friend can sell him her car for $4000. The down payment of 20% is $800, which his father will give him. The loan is for $3200. Because he has no credit record in the U.S., the bank will require a higher interest rate -- 14%. His monthly payment on his car will be $75 for five years. And his car insurance will be $200 a month.

Ashvin, age 19, came from India ten years ago with his family and has been driving for one year. He is a university student on a full scholarship. He has a part-time job on weekends in his family's jewelry store. His part-time salary is $150 a week. His parents will co-sign the loan; otherwise, he wouldn't pass bank qualifications. He lives with his family and they pay all of his expenses. The used car he wants to buy is $5800. The down payment is $1160 and the interest rate is 14% because he has no credit record. The monthly payment will be $150 and his car insurance will be $200 a month because of his age and short driving record.

(Top 5 car companies in U.S: Toyota, Ford, General Motors, Honda, Daimler Chrysler
Top three: Toyota, Honda, General Motors. Best selling car in U.S. : Toyota Camry)

Privacy
(Partial Dictation) dictation page 15 (cd track 5)

Operator:	Thank you for calling Pizza Castle. May I **have your order**?
Customer:	Hello, can I order....
Operator:	Can I have your multi-purpose **card number** first, sir?
Customer:	It's eh ..... hold on ..... 3122058889-31- **54610**.
Operator:	Okay... **you're** Mr. Saxe and **you're calling** from 26 Rose Lane. Your home number is 627-734-**2366**. Your office is 627-373-5716 and your mobile is 627-266-**2566**. Would you like to have this delivery made to 26 Rose Lane?
Customer:	Yes. How did you get all my phone numbers?
Operator:	We are connected **to the system**, sir.
Customer:	May I order your **Seafood Pizza**?
Operator:	That's **not a good idea**, sir.
Customer:	How come?
Operator:	**According to** your medical records, you have **high** blood pressure and even **higher** cholesterol level, sir.
Customer:	What do you recommend then?
Operator:	Try our low-fat soybean yogurt pizza. **You'll like it**.
Customer:	How do you **know for sure**?
Operator:	You **borrowed** a book titled "Popular Soybean Yogurt Dishes" from your local library last week, sir.
Customer:	Okay, I **give up**. Give me three family-sized ones, then. How much will that cost?
Operator:	That should be enough for **your family of ten**, sir. The total is **$49.99**.
Customer:	**Can I pay** by credit card?
Operator:	**I'm afraid that** you have to pay us cash, sir. Your credit card is over the limit and you've owed your bank **$3720.55** since October.
Customer:	I guess I'll have to run to the neighborhood ATM and **withdraw cash** before your guy arrives.

Operator: You can't do that, sir. Based on the records, **you've reached** your daily limit on machine withdrawal today.

Customer: **Never mind.** Just send the pizzas. I'll have the cash ready. **How long** is it going to take?

Operator: **About 45 minutes**, sir, but if you can't wait, you can always come and collect it on your motorcycle.

Customer: Wha.... !

Operator: **According to** the details in the system, you own a Harley, registration number E1123.

Customer: @#%&@#

Operator: Better watch your language, sir. Remember that on **May 9th** you were accused of using abusive language to an officer.

Customer: (Speechless)

Operator: Is there **anything else**?

Customer: Nothing. **By the way,** aren't you going to give me three bottles of Pepsi?

Operator: We normally would, sir, but based on your records, you're also **diabetic**.

Pocket Translators
(Dictogloss)
dictation page 19 (cd track 6)

1. Pocket translators are easier to use than bilingual dictionaries.

2. Pocket translators have both advantages and disadvantages.

3. Students use pocket translators too often in their ESL classrooms.

4. The students should rely on the teacher, not their translators.

5. You can use your pocket translator in a math class or a history class.

The Noblest of Professions
(Partial Dictation)
dictation page 21 (cd track 7)

1. A teacher is a guide in the **adventure of learning**.

2. A teacher is a **salesperson**. The product is **knowledge**.

3. A teacher is a **counselor**, a **nurse**, a healer of broken hearts.

4. A teacher is **so much more** than what a test can measure.

5. A teacher is a coach, a cheerleader, **and a peacemaker**.

6. A teacher is a psychiatrist fostering **self-esteem** and an optometrist helping students

   see clearly.

7. A teacher is an **actor**, a **comedian**, and a storyteller.

8. A teacher is an X-ray technician **reading minds**, a publisher at the copy machine,

   a partner **with parents** in the adventure of education.

Well-paid rankings (these vary from year to year)
1-airline pilot
2-surgeon
3-criminal lawyer
4-electrical engineer
**5-electricians, plumbers, and mail carriers all make about the same (no university degree
necessary)**
6-registered nurse
7-psychologist

Ten most dangerous jobs
1. **timber cutters**   2. **airplane pilots**   3. **construction laborers**   4. **truck drivers**
5. **farm occupations**   6. **groundskeepers**   7. **laborers**   8. **police and detectives**
9. **carpenters**   10. **sales occupations**

Opportunity Knocks
(Prediction Dictation)

dictation page 24 (cd track 8)

Most **high** schools will not accept young people who are **over** 17, have a history of school troubles, speak little **English**, or otherwise seem unlikely to be able **to pass** the final exams and graduate in a reasonable amount of **time**. **In** New York, a night **and** day school **was** created for these students.

Four **years** ago, just before his sixteenth **birthday**, Jean-Luc Gerard landed at Kennedy **Airport** with $20.00 in his **pocket**, alone, speaking no **English**, and traumatized by the deaths of his uncle and brother in a West African civil war. **His** mother **was** kidnapped, and he **never** saw her again.

Four **years** later Mr. Gerard **had** graduated from this high school with a full **scholarship** to Dartmouth College. He had been a night student while **working** full-time during the **day**. The teachers helped **him** with tutoring. They **taught** him English. They **helped** him with immigration and gave him a mentor. The mentor even gave him a party when he was **accepted** to college.

More than half of the students at the **school** are recent **immigrants** like Mr. Gerard. Most come to school during the day for intensive **English** classes after they have been turned down by other high schools because of their age. No one at the school has much **money.** Many students at the school hold some kind of **job** to support **themselves**, their children, and sometimes other family **members.**

Home Schooling
(Note Taking)
dictation page 28 (cd track 9)

Why did you choose home schooling for your daughter?

My husband and I were not happy with the education Eve was getting in the public schools, and we didn't want to send her to private school, which is too expensive and too far away. My husband and I believed that we could give Eve a better education at home, a place where she will be excited about learning and be challenged.

Is home schooling legal?

Yes, it is now, in every state. Back in the 1970s when conservative Christians wanted to home school their children for religious reasons, it was not really accepted by mainstream Americans. But in the 1980s and 90s it became more popular, not only for the religious right, but for thousands of parents like ourselves who felt we could do a better job than the public schools.

How does home schooling work?

When we first started this project, we copied the traditional classroom subjects, trying to improve on them. But we later tried other approaches which worked even better. We can buy lesson plans in all subjects from organizations and schools. We use the Internet for virtual courses offered by different schools, and we have joined a network of families called the HS Club, where we parents share our expertise and have support groups. Sometimes we hire tutors.

Do you and your husband have teaching degrees?

I graduated from a two-year college where I studied English, and my husband has a master's degree in engineering. I do most of the teaching during the day, but we have Eve do a lot of independent study on topics that interest her, and we take lots of field trips to museums.

Were you at all worried that Eve could become isolated from other children her age?

Actually, that was a concern in the beginning, but we have this network of activities that put home schoolers together. For example, in the HS Club we have a theater group, a problem-solving group, a ski group, a math club. We also have science fairs and music recitals. We get together often, and Eve has made many friends.

Discussion answers: ❖

Fact or Opinion? 1. Fact 2. Opinion 3. Fact 4. Opinion 5. Fact

True, False or IDK (I don't know)

1. False 2. True 3. False 4. True 5. IDK 6. True 7. False 8. IDK

A Success Story
(Note Taking)   *dictation page 31 (cd track 10)*

Tell me about your family and your childhood.

My family have been migrant workers for forty years. We spend half the year in Mexico and half the year moving around the West Coast picking crops like peaches, cherries, and olives. New immigrants who come to the country and work hard often are able to send their children to university and the second generation moves into the middle class, but this is not true for migrant workers. I grew up in the fields in America with my mother and father and sister. The work was hard, but the worst part was it was so boring.

What was your early schooling like?

My early schooling was very bad. I was in and out of schools because we were always moving. I wasn't interested in school, and I didn't do the homework that teachers often sent home with me.

I know that you did very well in high school. Can you tell us about it?

Somehow when I got to high school, I began to attend class full time. Really, my passion for learning came from my mother. She is very interested in everything. I became a very good student. I graduated second in the senior class and got a full scholarship to a good university in California.

Some unfortunate things have happened to you, as well. Can you talk about these?

A terrible thing happened in the summer between high school and college. My father and I were riding with other workers in a truck. We were heading home so that I could get ready to leave for my freshman year in college. My father was so proud of me and we were very happy. Suddenly a large trailer truck ran a stop sign and hit us. Five of the workers were killed. One was my father. I was one of the three that survived.

Please tell me about your university life and your plans for the future.

I went off to college with a heavy heart. Nothing at college was as hard as seeing my father dying. But his pride in me and my mother's belief in me kept me going. Finally I earned a degree in Civil Engineering. While I was there I met someone who had an MBA from Harvard. I applied to go there and couldn't believe that I was accepted.

When I got there, I had a hard time at first. American students are very self-confident and that's very important in business school. My culture teaches us to be quiet and not speak up even when we know the answer. I had to learn to speak up for myself. Now I want to start a Migrant Project that will make a difference and help other migrant students succeed. One of my first clients is my mother, who only had a third-grade education. She loves computers, and I am going to help her start an online business. If she is successful, she can stop her boring job canning peaches.

Underage Drinking
(Dictogloss)

dictation page 33 (cd track 11)

Introduction ✳

1. True: The legal drinking age in all 50 states is 21.
2. True/false — depending on the state. The legal driving age is different in each state.
   Check yours!
3. True
4. True

Dictogloss ✳

Dear Deena,

I am 17, and though I feel I am an adult, I can't afford to buy my own car, so I must use my parents'. They are good about lending it to me but are absolutely fanatic on the subject of drinking and driving. I know that drinking causes many accidents, but I also know that I can drive safely after drinking only two beers. How can I persuade my parents to see that it's okay?

George from Georgetown

(Students should point out that he's underage, that alcohol slows reaction time and gives one a false sense of invulnerability.)

Overprotected?
(Prediction)   *dictation page 35 (cd track 12)*

Dear Amy:

   I read you **on** the Internet because I **live** in Europe. I am **married** to a foreigner and **live** in his country; I love it here, but my problem is the difference in attitude about children.

   Specifically, I **have** a nine-year-old daughter who must take a bus to the train **station** and then a 20-minute **ride** on a train to get to her school. It is a private bilingual **school**.

   Many of the **children** in her **class** come from far **away** on their **own**. In fact, this is quite common in their culture. Children are off to school on their **own** as young **as** kindergarten.

   My husband and my daughter's teacher have been pressuring me; she **says** I am overprotective, that I should let my daughter make this trip **by herself**. I am just **not** comfortable with this. I am American and my instinct is to not allow a nine-year-old to go through a big city train **station** on **her own**. Am I overprotective? How can I ever **feel** comfortable about this?

                                            Kate

Driver's Licenses for Illegal Immigrants?
(Note Taking)   *dictation page 38 (cd track 13)*

Note: If this is the first note-taking activity your students have done, it would be good to do the first one (Karen Johnson) together to be sure they are only recording the important information.

1. Karen Johnson. No. Illegal immigrants should not have driver's licenses because they are criminals, and they are taking jobs away from Americans and legal immigrants.

2. Jason Garcia. Yes. If they can read and understand English enough to pass the written and road tests, they will understand the laws of the road. If we don't allow them to get a license, they will still drive and have accidents.

3. Helen Chen. No. Illegal immigrants should not have the same rights and privileges. If I commit an illegal act, my driver's license can be revoked. Illegal immigrants are committing an illegal act by coming here without permission.

4. David Peterson. No. The government should spend more money to help our older legal citizens get better medical coverage.

5. Susanne Roberts. Yes, but first the government should check their driving records in their own countries. They need to drive to work, and they need insurance, and they must follow the laws now that they are here.

6. Minnie Lee. No. There are too many people who have legal licenses and still do not know how to drive. There are too many crazy drivers on the roads. Illegal immigrants should go back home, NOW!

Fact or Opinion *(see page 39)*

1. O
2. F
3. O
4. O
5. F

Dear Mom and Dad
(Partial Dictation)

dictation page 42 (cd track 14)

Dear Mom and Dad,

Since I left for college, I **have been** very bad about writing, and I am sorry for my thought-lessness in not **having** written before. I will bring you up to date now, but before you read on, please sit down. You are not to read any further unless you are sitting down. Okay?

Well then, I am getting along pretty well now. The skull fracture and the concussion I got when I **jumped** out of the window of my dormitory when it **caught** on fire is pretty well **healed** now. I only **spent** two weeks in the hospital, and now I can see almost normally and only **get** these sick headaches once a day. Fortunately, the fire in my dormitory and my jump **were seen** by an attendant at the gas station near the dorm, and he was the one who **called** the fire department and the ambulance. He also **visited** me in the hospital, **brought me** flowers, and since then we **have fallen** in love. We are **about to** marry, and I **am leaving** the university in order to find a job. He is **divorced** and has three young children that he **must support**. This is difficult **to do** on a gas station attendant's salary, and I **must help.**

Correct Verb Tenses *(not on CD)*

I know that you will welcome him into our family with open arms. He is kind, and although not well educated he is ambitious. Although he is of a different race and religion than ours, I know you will not be be bothered by that.

Now that I have brought you up to date, I want to tell you that there was no dormitory fire. I did not have a concussion or skull fracture. I was not in the hospital and there is no boyfriend in my life. However, I am getting a D in history and F in science, and I want you to see those marks in their proper perspective.

Your loving daughter,

Susan

Bad Dog? Bad Owner?
(Partial Dictation)

dictation page 45 (cd track 15)

1. In a small town on Martha's Vineyard in Massachusetts, the town selectmen **had to make** a decision about Sabrina, a large dog **who had killed** and eaten several chickens belonging to a neighbor.

"I don't think we should be tolerating this," said **one of the** selectmen. "**I've lost** some chickens to dogs myself, and I think a vicious dog **that attacks animals** should be destroyed."

What was unusual about this situation was that the owner **of the chickens** found dog hairs in the chicken house. He took hairs from three of his neighbors' dogs **and sent them** to a DNA lab. Sabrina's was a **perfect match**.

The woman in the lab said that this was the first time **she had helped** convict a four-legged killer.

2. Mrs. Minami lives in a pretty house with a garden that she **is proud of.** Her next-door neighbor, Mr. Sampson, has a twelve-year-old son, Ralph, **who has a dog** named Storm. He often lets Storm **out of the house** on her own. Storm likes to go into Mrs. Minami's garden and **dig holes** and **eat flowers.** Mrs. Minami **has spoken** twice to Mr. Sampson and to Ralph, but **nothing has changed.**

3. Jeffrey had agreed **to watch** Buffy, a poodle, for a weekend because his good friends, the Cogans, were going to a family wedding. After **they came back**, and Buffy had gone home, Jeffrey's wife found their eleven-year-old's **very expensive** dental retainer on the floor **with a dog bite** in it. It will cost approximately $500.00 **to replace**.

Bullies
(Partial Dictation)   *dictation page 48 (cd track 16)*

Case One. Elementary School

Billy was a **ten-year-old** fifth grader who was **walking home** from school one day. In front of him were **three smaller girls.** Billy began picking on them, so the girls **reported him** to their teacher the next day. The teacher then punished Billy by having him **stay after school** and clean the boards and perform other menial chores. Billy's parents **were angry with** the punishment. They felt that because the incident happened after school, it was not **the school's problem.**

Case Two. Middle School

Rosie goes to a program **in her school** called ROPES, which stands for "Respect Other People Equally Siempre." The program **is supposed to** help stop bullying, but Rosie still has problems with one girl, Linda, who picks on her for **no special reason.** Lately, Linda has been teasing her **even more**. She is hurt by the bad names she calls her, and the situation is getting so bad that she **is thinking of** suicide. Her friends say that Linda bullies her because **she gets bullied herself,** but Rosie sees no reason for Linda to make fun of her.

Case Three. High School

Robert **got into a fight** in school with another boy named Charles. Charles started the fight and was often teasing and shoving Robert **in the hallways.** During the fight, Charles pulled off Robert's **gold chain** and kept it. He refused to return it. Robert **is afraid to** complain to his teacher because he **doesn't speak English very well.**

How Honest Are You?
(Pair dictation)   *dictation page 51 (cd track 17)*

Note: Tell the students to write out the figures in millions, i.e., thirty-three, not 33. They should also use the % sign, not write it out.

According to an article in the New York Times on January 8, 2004, titled "Never Lost But Found Daily: Japanese Honesty," if you lost a $100 bill in Tokyo, there is a good chance that it would be returned, and you could claim it.

In Tokyo, with eight million people in the city and thirty-three million in the metropolitan area, a $100 bill would probably find its way to the Tokyo Metropolitan Police Lost and Found Center.

In 2002, people found and brought to the Tokyo Center twenty-three million in cash. 72% of it was returned to the owners once they had persuaded the police it was theirs. About 19% went to the finders after no one claimed the money for half a year.

Children are taught from early on to hand in anything they find to the police in their neighborhood.

The most frequently lost item is umbrellas, 360,000 in 2002. The item with the highest rate of return is the cell phone, 75%.

Do people in your city return things they find? Do you?

Subway Manners
dictation page 54 (cd track 18)
(Partial Dictation)

1. When reading your newspaper, keep it **within** your own personal space. Don't block another's personal space. Take your paper with you when you leave the train. **Don't leave it behind** on the seat.

2. Please don't let **your cell phone** ring, or worse yet, play **a silly little song**. Research indicates that one of the **most annoying noises** is being forced to listen to someone's one-sided cell phone conversation.

3. Avoid eating **smelly, messy,** or **sticky** food on a train. The **sight, sound,** and **smell** are off-putting to those around you.

4. Avoid computer or gaming sounds on your electronic devices. Again, noises are irritating to **other passengers.**

5. If you must **cough or sneeze**, lower your head and cover your mouth with a tissue to avoid spreading your germs to those **around you**.

6. Help passengers who may need help **on or off** the train, and **offer your seat** to a senior citizen or pregnant woman.

7. Avoid staring **at other travelers.** You may not even be conscious of staring.

Rights and Responsibilities of Citizenship
(Partial Dictation) *dictation page 57 (cd track 19)*

Right **1.**   You **will be able to** vote in national, state, and local elections.

Right **2.**   If you want, you **could run for** political office or hold a government job.

Resp. **3.**   You **should vote** in all elections.

Resp. **4.**   You **are supposed to** show up for jury duty.

Right **5.**   You **could volunteer** to serve in the armed forces.

Resp. **6.**   If you work, you **will have to** pay federal income taxes.

Resp. **7.**   You **ought to** become a well-informed citizen by reading the newspaper.

Fact or Opinion? *(see page 58)*

1. F
2. O
3. O
4. F

Non-English Speakers in the US
(Dictogloss) *dictation page 60 (cd track 20)*

1. Nearly one in five Americans speak a language other than English at home. **(13)**

2. 47 million Americans older than five used a language besides English in 2000. **(13)**

3. Most speak Spanish or Chinese. **(5)**

4. The Spanish-speaking population rose by 62 percent. **(8)**

5. Hispanics are now the largest minority group in the U.S. **(10)**

Yard Sales
(Prediction) dictation page 62 (cd track 21)

Carol and Alan **have been** married **for** 25 years. It is a good marriage and they **are** happy. **But** there is one problem; Alan is a pack rat. He **never** throws anything away. He **reads** two newspapers every day and keeps most of them around the house in case he wants to reread an article. Most of the **time** he never does.

He is also addicted to yard **sales,** and almost every weekend he comes **home** with several things. For instance, he often **buys** toys for a day in the future when he has a grandchild. He also **buys** broken chairs that he plans to **fix** one day in the **future**. He never **throws** anything out. The house is becoming more and **more** crowded with things that are never used.

Carol, on the other **hand**, throws **away** anything she is sure she will never use again. When Alan is **out** of the house, she **throws** away lots of newspapers and some other **things**. Once when he asked where something she had thrown **out** was, she **said,** "I have no idea where it can be."

Amy Tan, Writer

dictation page 66 (cd track 22)

(Partial Dictation)

Introduction ❀

(7)   1.   In 1987, at age 35, Amy first visited China with her elderly mother. The trip changed her life.

(2)   2.   When she was a child, Amy's parents expected her to become a doctor and a concert pianist.

(5)   3.   After receiving her bachelor's and master's degrees from San Jose State, she enrolled in a doctoral program at UC Berkeley.

(4)   4.   Amy's mother enrolled her in a Baptist college in CA to study pre-med but Amy rebelled and followed her boyfriend to San Jose State University, where she studied English and linguistics.

(1)   5.   Amy was born in Oakland, California, in 1952.

(3)   6.   When Amy's father and brother both died of brain tumors within a year, Amy and her mother and her other brother moved to Switzerland, where Amy finished high school.

(6)   7.   In 1974, Amy married Louis DeMattei, an attorney who practiced tax law.

(9)   8.   Today, Ms. Tan continues to write not only novels but also children's books.

(8)   9.   The trip allowed Amy to see where her mother's roots came from and was the inspiration for Amy to complete stories she had started writing at home.

Dictation ❀

First, I would say to them, you **are not alone**. I thought I was (in the 50s and 60s), and I **didn't realize it** until I wrote *The Joy Luck Club*. I had so many readers who said, "I feel as though you've **written my life**." A lot of young people come up to me and say, "I feel the same way, and I still feel that way. I don't get along with my mother and I'm the only kid in an **all-white community**. And I don't know **if I'm Chinese**. Am I American? Am I Korean? What should I be? How should I feel about this?"

It's **hard to believe**, but this feeling changes over time. It's normal to **feel conflicted**. What you'll find later on is that **this whole question** of who you are is a very, very interesting question, and having two cultures to add **to the mix** of it makes it even more interesting. If you ever have a chance **to go back** to the country of your parents or your ancestors, you'll find out, not how Chinese or Korean or Indian you are, you'll find out **how American you are**. This will give you a sense of perspective and humor that will help you find your own identity.

Thanksgiving
(Partial Dictation) *dictation page 69 (cd track 23)*

Fact 1. Thanksgiving always comes on the **fourth Thursday** in November.

Op. 2. It is the **most loved** American holiday.

Fact 3. Many people have a big dinner that includes **turkey** and **pumpkin pie.**

Op. 4. Turkey is tastier **than chicken**.

Op. 5. Thanksgiving dinners are **a lot of work** to prepare.

Fact 6. The Pilgrims started this tradition of **giving thanks** in 1621.

Fact 7. They came to Plymouth, Massachusetts, in 1620 to find **religious freedom.**

Fact 8. They came **in the winter** and didn't have enough food to eat.

Fact 9. **The Indians** helped them by giving them food and showing them how **to farm.**

Fact 10. At the end of their first year in America, the Pilgrims **invited the** Indians to celebrate with a **big dinner** in appreciation for their help in surviving their first year.

Fact 11. Thanksgiving is **the busiest** travel holiday of the year. Airports are **crowded.**

A Tour of Washington, D.C.
(Prediction Dictation)

dictation page 72 (cd track 24)

Good morning, ladies and **gentlemen**, boys and **girls**. My name is George, and I am

your personal tour guide. For the **next** six hours, we **will** be exploring exciting

Washington, D.C., the **capital** of the United States. Let's start off with a bang and visit the

White House, D.C.'s **most** popular tourist attraction. Who knows, **maybe** we'll even get

to **see** the president at work in the Oval Office. Then it's only a hop, skip, and a jump to

the Smithsonian Institute where you **could** probably spend a whole week, there's so

much to **see**. Then it's on to the Lincoln Memorial. If you ask 100 Americans who the

greatest **president** of the U.S. was, most will say Abraham Lincoln. That's because he

signed the Emancipation Proclamation to free the slaves. And here's the Big One! For

lunch, we're **going** to the Capitol Building Cafeteria, where you'll get to **meet** famous

politicians like Senator Ted Kennedy. You may even ask them to sign their autographs for

the low, low, low price of $50. HA! HA! HA! All aboard!

Little People of America
(Partial Dictation)
dictation page 75 (cd track 25)

R: I understand there are about **1500 people** at this conference.

A: Yes. Some of the younger little people come **with their parents**, who are of average stature.

R: What are **the causes** of dwarfism?

A: It is a chemical change within a **single gene** that begins during conception. It is not caused by anything the parents have done during pregnancy **or before**. Nine out of ten children born with this condition have **average-sized parents**.

R: Are there **different types of** dwarfism?

A: Yes, but the most **common form** is called achondroplasia, which accounts for **70%** of all cases.

R: Is dwarfism **a disability**?

A: We **don't want to be** considered disabled, although some of us have spinal and orthopedic problems. Most of us have **normal intelligence**, normal life spans, and reasonably good health.

R: Coming to a conference like this is **a great way** to socialize with others like yourself.

A: Yeah, it's wonderful because here I can find people who understand the **day-to-day** things I experience. At least **one time a year**, I get to feel normal. People here instantly connect and it's like, "wow!" You could actually meet someone for a **long-term** relationship.

R: What kinds of activities **are there**?

A: There are workshops for our **relatives and friends** who want to learn more about our condition. Medical specialists **provide counseling** on topics like neurological concerns, pregnancy, and psychological **issues**.

R: I see that there are other fun activities as well.

A: Uh, huh. There are **fashion shows**, dances, soccer games, and typical tourist trips to **interesting places.**

R: What's the best part for you?

A: The **people you meet** and exchange e-mails with. I'm definitely going **to check out** the guy scene. Who knows, I may find someone **short, dark**, and handsome!

Note: The book, *Little People: Learning to See the World Through My Daughter's Eyes*, by Dan Kennedy; Rodale Publishers, is an excellent chronicle of a father whose daughter is a dwarf. We recommend it!

The First Americans
(Partial Dictation)

dictation page 79 (cd track 26)

Archeologists believe Native Americans came from **Asia** 25,000 years ago. By the year **5000 B.C.**, many different groups lived **in all parts** of North America. Because Indians lived in scattered groups and **had little contact** with each other, they developed **different cultures**. They spoke **over 1000** different languages, **wore** different types **of clothing**, built different **types of homes,** and made **their living** in different ways. Those who settled in the northern areas **hunted and fished**. Those who settled in the **east and southwest** farmed. Despite their many differences, most Indians **shared the belief** that people should live in harmony **with nature.** They believed that people should not **own land** because the land, like the air, stars, and water, belonged **to everyone**. The European settlers believed in the ownership of **private property**. These two very different **ways of life** were the basis of the many conflicts between the Indians and the settlers.

In the early years of discovery and exploration between **1492** and the mid **1600s**, relations with the Indians were, for the most part, **friendly**. But as more and more settlers arrived, **conflicts developed.** Indian tribal leaders were **worried and angry** because settlers were crowding people off their land. When Indians "sold" land to the settlers, the Indians **misunderstood and thought** they were only giving whites the right to use the land.

Many settlers **tried to understand** the Indian way of life and **treat them fairly.** But others cheated them and took their land. While Indians always fought **for their rights**, they were unable to stop the advance of thousands of settlers supported by the **U.S. Army**. Indians won some battles, but they always **ended up** losing their lands.

By **1880**, fighting had stopped. Finally, the government moved almost all the remaining Indians **onto reservations.** Today, however, **less than half** of the Indians live on reservations. Those who do, try to preserve their **tribal customs** and ways of life. But discrimination by non-Indians, an unwillingness by Indians to **adopt new ways**, and a basic **distrust of** the federal government, have kept many Indians out of the **mainstream** of **modern** life.

We Shall Overcome
(Partial Dictation)

dictation page 82 (cd track 27)

We shall overcome   Deep in my heart
We shall overcome   I do believe
We shall overcome some day.   We shall overcome some day.

Although President Abraham Lincoln's Emancipation Proclamation set the slaves free during **the Civil War** in 1865, blacks **in the 1950s**, especially in the south, still suffered from unfair treatment because of **their race**. Some states did not allow blacks **to vote**. Schools, buses, trains, and public businesses like theaters and restaurants were segregated — separated into facilities for **blacks and whites.**

Imagine being a **black man, woman,** or child in 1950 in Mississippi. You **could not vote.** You could go to school with black children only. You could drink only from a separate water fountain, use separate bathrooms, swim in a separate swimming pool, and ride at the **back of the bus**.

In the 40s and 50s, Presidents Roosevelt and Truman had said that discrimination based on race and religion was against the ideals of **American democracy**. However, it was not until 1954 that the Supreme Court said, "Separate educational facilities are inherently unequal." With this ruling, the Civil Rights Movement **was born**. The courts ordered schools to be desegregated.

Now blacks had government support in their fight for equality, and the Civil Rights Movement **had begun**. It took ten years before the Civil Rights Act was passed by Congress. During that time many black citizens were holding peaceful marches and sit-ins **in order to** get voting rights and desegregated schools. They were often violently attacked by whites and even policemen armed with batons, bullwhips, fire hoses, **and dogs.** But still they marched peacefully, singing "We Shall Overcome" while the world watched **on television**.

The song "We Shall Overcome," **adapted from** a black gospel song, became the song of the **Civil Rights** Movement. It was sung during the sit-ins, voter registration drives, and protest marches of those heroic days. Since that time this song **has been sung** by people **all over** the world who are fighting for equality or **for freedom**.

Note to Teachers: This lesson can be used at any time, but it is particularly appropriate before Martin Luther King, Jr. Day in January. It is most effective if the teacher plays/teaches the song, and students sing it.

Complaining
(Partial Dictation)   dictation page 84 (cd track 29)

1. The food at McDonald's **isn't very good.**

2. **English grammar** is illogical.

3. There are **so many immigrants** in the U.S.

4. It's been raining for **six straight days.**

5. American cars **are gas guzzlers.**

6. I have to pay a lot **for medical insurance.**

7. My parents **are too strict.**

What's So Funny?
(Pair dictation)   dictation page 88 (cd track 29)

Joke 1: "Those people upstairs are very annoying," complained the tenant. "Last night they stomped and banged on the floor until midnight." "Did they wake you?" asked the landlord. "No," replied the tenant. "Luckily, I was playing my tuba."

Joke 2: As a senior citizen was driving down the highway, his car phone rang. Answering, he heard his wife's voice urgently warning him. "Herman, I just heard on the news that there's a car going the wrong way on Route 280. I know you usually take Route 280, so please be careful!" "Yikes," yelled Herman, "it's not just ONE car. It's hundreds of them!"

Proverbs
(Partial Dictation)   *dictation page 91 (cd track 30)*

1. There's no **place like home**.

2. Don't **count your chickens** before they're hatched.

3. First **come**, first **served**.

4. Love makes the world **go round**.

5. **Time** is **money.**

6. **Too many cooks** spoil the broth.

7. You can't **teach an old dog** new tricks.

8. You can't have your cake and **eat it too**.

9. **Live** and **learn.**

10. The **early bird** catches the worm.

11. The **first step** is the hardest.

12. The apple doesn't **fall very far** from the tree.

Brain Teasers
dictation page 94 (cd track 31)
(Partial Dictation)

1. Which is heavier, a pound of feathers, or a **pound of cement**? (they weigh the same)

2. How many **birth days** does the average person have?   (one)

3. Can a man **who is living** in northern United States be buried in Canada?
   (no, he's still living – alive)

4. A little girl is playing **at the beach**. She is making sand piles. She has **three piles** in one
   place and **four piles** in another place. If she puts them **all together,** how many sand piles
   will she have?   (one)

5. Bob **is standing behind** Sam. Sam is standing behind Bob at the **same time.** How is that
   possible?   (They are standing back to back.)

6. **Would you rather** have a lion attack *you* or a tiger?   (You have to read this with the
   emphasis on the word "you" so that your answer would be, "I'd rather have the lion
   attack the tiger.")

7. What word, if pronounced right, **is wrong**, but if pronounced wrong **is right**? (wrong)

8. Do you know the thing that has keys that open **no doors,** has space but **no room**, and allows
   you to enter but **not go in**?   (a keyboard)

Riddle answers: 1. C; 2. D; 3. B; 4. A

Note: This is a fun activity to do after a "real" test. It's a good way to release tension!

Trivia Contest
(Partial Dictation)

dictation page 96 (cd track 32)

1. What does the abbreviation ET **stand for?** (extra terrestrial)

2. What do people put **French, Russian,** and **Italian** dressing on? (salads)

3. What is the **greatest number of babies** that a woman has had at one time? (8)

4. What do people in the United States have to do **on April 15**? (file and pay income tax)

5. What is the name of the **traditional woman's dress** in India? (sari)

6. What do you do when you **grab a bite**? (You get something to eat.)

7. Who wrote **A Christmas Carol**? (Charles Dickens)

8. What sports event takes place **on a diamond?** (baseball)

9. Which is the **largest continent**? (Asia)

10. What **language** do they speak in **Brazil**? (Portuguese)

11. What is present in **tea, coffee, soda,** and chocolate? (caffeine)

12. What was the **first American college** and where **is it located?** (Harvard, Cambridge, MA)

13. Who does a car with the **initials MD** on the license plate **belong to**? (a doctor)

14. Who was both **deaf** and **blind,** but became a **writer**? (Helen Keller)

Cooperative Learning Answers

Group 1: January, sandwiches, diamond, ear, Shakespeare

Group 2: soccer, interesting (exciting), alligator, Chinese, ice cream

Group 3: ten, carbonated drinks, Bible, electronic mail, approximately 2 million

Group 4: cockroach, money, unidentified flying object, Siam, thirteen

What's in a Name?
(Partial Dictation)

dictation page 99 (cd track 33)

"What's in a name?" wrote Shakespeare. "A rose by any other name would smell as sweet." **Nevertheless**, we give great importance to names. In some **cultures** the baby **is given** the name of a favorite **relative** who has died. In other **cultures**, the first-born **male** child receives the same name as his father with one **small difference**. In an English-speaking culture, if the father is Wilson Smith, Sr. (Senior), the baby becomes Wilson Smith, Jr. (Junior). When Wilson Smith, Jr., has a baby, that baby may be called Wilson Smith, III (the third).

Some people name their children after **movie stars** or famous people. In the 1940s many girls named Shirley **were named** after a child actress, Shirley Temple. Nowadays we **often meet** children named Celine and Brad.

When people from other **countries** come to the United States, **either** as international students or as **immigrants**, they often change their names and **adopt** English names. They do this for **several** reasons. First, English speakers may have **difficulty** understanding and **pronouncing** their names correctly. Second, people may have **trouble remembering** their names. Third, because they are in a new country, they may want to change their **lives** and begin with a new name.

In a recent discussion among ESL teachers, one teacher said, "For Koreans, names are incredibly **important,** not to be thrown **away** lightly, and we are not doing right by our Korean students if we encourage them to **adopt** English names. It is a form of **respect** to learn the Korean names correctly." Another teacher responded, "I have a problem with Korean and Chinese names. They all seem to be three syllables. They are not **clearly** identifiable to me as **male** or **female.** Korean names are so similar that I cannot **keep them** apart in my mind for at least the first four or five weeks of class, no matter **how hard I try**. I know who the students are. I just **mix up** their names."

Home Remedies
(Partial Dictation)   *dictation page 101 (cd track 34)*

It is just fermented cabbage, garlic, and chili peppers, **but Asians** are buying **record amounts** of kimchi, hoping Korea's **national dish** is really a wonder drug. Southeast Asians are **stocking up** on it. It's very **popular** in China. And South Koreans, **who eat it** with every meal, are buying more than usual, hoping that word of its curative powers will make it famous.

"**I can't imagine** a meal without kimchi," said a housewife. "**I'm making** my children **eat** a lot more of it these days. I certainly believe that they did not get SARS because they eat **a lot of kimchi.**"

A Korean scientist says this theory may be difficult to prove, but that doesn't mean **it doesn't work.**

Chocoholics, Unite!
(Partial Dictation)   *dictation page 103 (cd track 35)*

Op. 1. Chocolate from Belgium **is the best.**

Fact 2. People crave chocolate more than **any other food.**

Fact 3. Chocolate **consists of chemicals** associated with mood, emotion, and addiction.

Op 4. Chocolate is sinful because it has lots of **fat and calories.**

Fact 5. Chocolate lovers **have been around** for almost 3000 years.

Fact 6. Chocolate comes from cacao beans, and **in ancient times** was used as a form of currency.

Fact 7. **You can find** cacao trees in Africa, Southeast Asia, and South and Central America.

Op 8. You can **enjoy chocolate more** when you are depressed or stressed.

Note to teachers: **This works well when you give students some chocolate before or after the lesson!**

Eat that Insect?
(Pair dictaton)   *dictation page 106 (cd track 36)*

Ladybugs are cute and butterflies are pretty, but most people who come face to face with an insect have one thought: Step on it! David Gordon takes a different approach. He cooks bugs and eats them. He thinks insects are a valuable, underused, and delicious source of nutrition. "If you're eating hot dogs, you're eating stuff that's way weirder than a grasshopper," said Gordon as he demonstrated his cooking skills in an elementary school cafeteria. On his grill he prepared grasshopper kebabs, fried crickets, and grilled mealworms. School rules prevented the children from eating bugs, but teachers tried them and thought they were tasty! But beware! Not all bugs taste good, and some are poisonous, especially caterpillars. Even birds and other animals do not want to eat them, which is why some caterpillars can eat and destroy thousands of trees each year.

What Do You Eat?
(Partial Dictation)

dictation page 111 (cd track 37)

Breakfast. During the work week, <u>**two-thirds**</u> of Americans eat breakfast, <u>**three-fourths**</u> of them at home. About <u>**one in five**</u> eats breakfast at work: <u>**one in ten**</u> while driving or commuting. The most popular breakfast is <u>**hot or cold**</u> cereal (67%), followed by <u>**toast**</u>, or muffins, or bagels **(55%)**, and eggs **(31%)**. <u>**Two-thirds**</u> also snack on cereal, and <u>**29%**</u> admit they eat cereal for dinner...sometimes.

Weekends. On <u>**Saturday**</u> and Sunday, <u>**87%**</u> of us eat breakfast at home. Eggs are the <u>**favorite**</u> Sunday breakfast for more than <u>**half.**</u>   Bacon, ham, or sausages are nearly as <u>**popular**</u>; so are pancakes or waffles.

Lunch. Sandwiches <u>**are popular**</u> at midday. <u>**Seven**</u> in <u>**ten**</u> of us put our food between two <u>**slices**</u> of bread. <u>**One in three**</u> eats <u>**fast food**</u>.

Dinner. About <u>**eight in ten**</u> who bring home <u>**takeout**</u> food said they prefer everything ready-to-eat, rather than also having a side dish prepared at home. <u>**Pizza**</u> is the favorite food-to-go (the choice of <u>**79%**</u>) followed by <u>**Chinese**</u> food (<u>**51%**</u>) and <u>**fast food**</u> such as hamburgers or tacos (<u>**40%**</u>).

Snacks. Evening is <u>**prime time**</u> for snackers. Nearly <u>**two-thirds**</u> of Americans snack after dinner (<u>**usually**</u> in front of the <u>**TV**</u>), and <u>**15%**</u> nibble all day long.

Save Our Planet Award
(Partial Dictation)

dictation page 114 (cd track 38)

1. The Teen Team. This **group of students** from Greenland Middle School saw a TV show about how plastic trash on beaches and **in the ocean** kills a million sea birds and fish every year. They organized a group of 15 student volunteers to **collect bottles**, plastic bags, and plastic containers from their city's beaches every month. This has **saved the lives** of many birds and fish.

2. Erin Brockton. Erin and her children discovered that **a paper company** in Greenland had been dumping poisonous chemicals in an **empty yard** near her neighborhood. Some of the poison had leaked into the reservoir where the town gets its **drinking water**. Many people got sick. After months **of complaining**, Erin forced the paper company to find other, safer ways **to get rid of** the waste.

3. VFR (Volunteers for Recycling). These people spend a lot of time at **the city dump.** Because they want to help Greenland residents **recycle their newspapers**, bottles, and cans. They also organized a "swap shop" at the dump where people could leave **old but good chairs,** TVs, computers, and other **useful things**. Then, people who need them can get them free. Their work has saved the town **thousands of dollars.**

4. Ray Burrows and Arthur Clark are biologists **who work at** the Greenland Labs. Burrows and Clark believe that pesticides **can cause cancer.** They want farmers to stop using chemical pesticides on their **vegetables and fruits.** They are getting farmers **to start using** insects that eat the insects that eat farmers' vegetables and fruits.

5. The Green Group. A group of adults and teens learned that many people in the city were dumping **dangerous materials** down the drain in their homes and into the sewer system. This is serious because it pollutes the city's **groundwater.** Many people can get sick from drinking water **that is polluted** from the dumping of motor oil, oven cleaners, **paint thinners**, and other dangerous chemicals. The Green Group organized two "hazardous waste" days a year at **the city dump**, where citizens can leave their products.

Venus and Serena Williams, Tennis Stars
(Dictogloss)

dictation page 118 (cd track 39)

1. Venus and Serena were first coached by their father. **(9)**

2. The sisters practiced tennis for up to six hours a day. **(10)**

3. Their father hoped that one day they would rule the professional tennis world. **(13)**

4. In 1999 Venus earned $4.6 million dollars. **(7)**

5. Although the sisters are rivals, they are also close friends. **(10)**

Alex Rodriguez, Baseball Player
(Dictogloss)

dictation page 120 (cd track 40)

1. Alex was born in New York in 1975. **(7)**

2. He grew up in Miami, where he loved to play baseball. **(11)**

3. Baseball managers began noticing him in high school when his team won a national championship. **(15)**

4. At age 18, he became one of the youngest players ever to play in the major leagues. **(17)**

5. He is a power hitter and an acrobatic fielder. **(9)**

6. In a typical season he can hit 52 home runs. **(10)**

Lacrosse
(Partial Dictation)
dictation page 122 (cd track 41)

F   1. Lacrosse is played **with a stick**, the crosse,

and the players need to know how

to **throw, catch** , and scoop.

F   2. Lacrosse is a fast-paced sport and **full of action**.

O   3. **Women are better players** than men because they are more agile.

F   4. Most lacrosse players play for **love of the sport** rather than for financial reward.

O   5. Women's lacrosse is the best sport **on the planet.**

O   6. Lacrosse is **a violent sport.**

F   7. Professional lacrosse in the U.S. has different rules and **is played indoors.**

Answers to chronology in Introduction

5, 1, 6, 2, 3, 7, 4

Violent Sports or Violent Fans?
(Partial Dictation)   *dictation page 125 (cd track 42)*

Case 1

A "hockey dad" **got into** an argument with the coach of his **son's team**. The argument led to **a serious fight** after the game. The hockey dad was so angry that he brutally attacked the coach. The coach died **the next day** from the injuries he suffered. There were many witnesses to the fight. The hockey dad **went to court**. What kind of punishment do you think **he should receive?**

Case 2

When a football team won the Super Bowl, there was **a big celebration** in their home city. **Thousands** of happy people were in the streets. Many had been drinking, however, and the crowd got **out of control.** People started overturning cars parked along the streets. One car owner, a university student, was afraid that his car would be destroyed **by the crowd,** so he got in his car and tried to **speed away**. In his nervous condition, he didn't see a student **crossing the street.** He hit the student and the student died. **The car owner** went to court. This is a case of manslaughter. **What kind of** punishment do you think he should receive?

Movie: Bend It Like Beckham
(Partial Dictation)

dictation page 127 (cd track 43)

Bend It Like Beckham is **the story of** a young Indian immigrant, Jess Bhamra, who lives in London with her protective and **traditional family.** She plays soccer for fun in a park with her friends, and Beckham **is her hero**. She is a talented **soccer player** in her own right, but her parents have other plans for their **youngest daughter.** They expect Jess to follow in the footsteps of her sister, Pinky, who is **preparing to marry** in a traditional Indian wedding.

Early in the film, Jess meets Jules, a girl her age who plays for a local **female soccer team.** Jules thinks Jess would be a good teammate and asks Jess to join up. Jess agrees and **quickly shows everyone** that she is a star player. But she doesn't **tell her parents** because she knows they would not approve. As a team member, she **makes new friends** and competes in out-of-town games that **take her out of** her small, restricted world.

To add romantic interest, both Jess and Jules **fall in love** with their young soccer coach. As the movie progresses, Jess has to **decide for herself** if she should follow her parents' wishes or live her life on **her own terms**. It is a delightful coming-of-age film which also allows us to look at **Indian culture in England.**

✳ *Other books from Pro Lingua* ✳
AT THE INTERMEDIATE AND ADVANCED LEVELS

Dictations for Discussion (*also by Judy DeFilippo and Catherine Sadow*)
Over 50 dictation activities in four different formats on a wide range of topics: Cultural Trends, Money and Work, Holidays and Special Events, Ethics, Health, and Language Facts and Fun. The readings range in difficulty from intermediate to advanced and they are in general somewhat longer than those in *Interactive Dictations*.

Discussion Strategies — Carefully structured pair and small group work at the advanced-intermediate level. Excellent preparation for students who will participate in academic or professional work that requires effective participation in discussion and seminars.

Conversation Strategies — 24 structured pair activities for developing strategic conversation skills at the intermediate level. Students learn the words, phrases, and conventions used by native speakers in active, give-and-take, everyday conversation.

Writing Strategies: A Student-Centered Approach — Two texts jam-packed with writing activities. Each covers four modes of writing. Book One (*Advanced Intermediate*) teaches • Description, • Narration, • Exposition, and • Comparison and Contrast. Book Two (*Advanced*) covers • Process, • Cause and Effect, • Extended Definition, and • Argumentation. Coordinated with these lessons are Fluency Writing Exercises and lessons on Grammar Problems and Terminology.

Write for You — A teacher resource book with copyable handouts. The focus is on creative activities that lead to effective writing by intermediate students who are intending to further their education.

Pearls of Wisdom — At the heart of this integrated skills builder are twelve stories from Africa and the Caribbean, collected and told by Dr. Raouf Mama of Benin. There is a student text for reading/listening, a workbook for discussion/vocabulary building, and two cassettes or CDs.

The Modal Book – 14 units explore the form, meaning, and use of the American English modal verb system, one semantic grouping at a time.

A Phrasal Verb Affair – over 200 phrasal verbs are presented and practiced in the context of a 15-episode soap opera. A dramatic reading on CD is available.

Shenanigames — Grammar-focused, interactive ESL activities and games providing practice with a full range of grammar structures. Photocopyable.

Getting a Fix on Vocabulary — A student text and workbook that focuses on affixation— building words by adding prefixes and suffixes to a root.

Lexicarry — Pictures for Learning Languages the Active Way. Over 4500 everyday words and expressions in 192 contexts that make conversation and interactive learning easy. There is a special new section on proverbs and sayings. Lots of words, even for very advanced students Additional material at www.Lexicarry.com.